STRAY

BY R. JOHNS

CURRENCY Press • Sydney

CURRENT THEATRE SERIES

First published in 2014
by Currency Press Pty Ltd,
PO Box 2287, Strawberry Hills, NSW, 2012, Australia
enquiries@currency.com.au
www.currency.com.au

in association with La Mama Theatre

Stray copyright © R. Johns, 2014

COPYING FOR EDUCATIONAL PURPOSES

The Australian *Copyright Act 1968* (Act) allows a maximum of one chapter or 10% of this book, whichever is the greater, to be copied by any educational institution for its educational purposes provided that that educational institution (or the body that administers it) has given a remuneration notice to Copyright Agency Limited (CAL) under the Act.

For details of the CAL licence for educational institutions contact CAL, Level 15, 233 Castlereagh Street, Sydney, NSW, 2000. Tel: within Australia 1800 066 844 toll free; outside Australia +61 2 9394 7600; Fax: +61 2 9394 7601; Email: info@copyright.com.au

COPYING FOR OTHER PURPOSES

Except as permitted under the Act, for example a fair dealing for the purposes of study, research, criticism or review, no part of this book may be reproduced, stored in a retrieval system, or transmitted in any form or by any means without prior written permission. All enquiries should be made to the publisher at the address above.

Any performance or public reading of *Stray* is forbidden unless a licence has been received from the author or the author's agent. The purchase of this book in no way gives the purchaser the right to perform the play in public, whether by means of a staged production or a reading. All applications for public performance should be addressed to the author c/– Currency Press.

NATIONAL LIBRARY OF AUSTRALIA CIP DATA

Title: Stray and The parricide / R Johns and Diane Stubbings.
ISBN: 9781925005097 (paperback)
Series: Current theatre series.
Other Authors/Contributors:
    Johns, R. Stray.
    Stubbings, Diane. The Parricide.

Cover design by Peter Mumford.

Currency Press acknowledges the Traditional Owners of the Country on which we live and work. We pay our respects to all Aboriginal and Torres Strait Islander Elders, past and present.

Contents

STRAY

R. Johns   1

Theatre Program at the end of the playtext

All knowledge, the totality of all questions and answers is contained in the dog.
Franz Kafka, *Investigations of a Dog*

...the poor dog, in life the firmest friend,
The first to welcome, foremost to defend.
Lord Byron, *Inscription on a Newfoundland Dog*

...dogs possess something very like a conscience.
Charles Darwin, *The Descent of Man*

Stray was funded through a creative development from Big West in 2012. *Stray* had its first public showing at The Workshop, Newport Substation December 2012.

Stray was first produced by the Big West Festival at Newport Substation, Melbourne, on 27 November 2013 with the following cast:

ACTOR ONE	John Shearman
ACTOR TWO	Ngaire Dawn Fair
ACTOR THREE	Trent Baker

Director, Kat Henry
Set Design and Graphics, Peter Mumford
Lighting Design, Kara Stacey Merrin
Production/Stage Manager, Kylie Russell
Audiovisuals, Brett Ludeman
Sound, ZackLee

Stray was first produced by La Mama Theatre, Melbourne, at La Mama Courthouse on 12 March 2014 with the following cast:

ACTOR ONE	Matt Whitty
ACTOR TWO	Ngaire Dawn Fair
ACTOR THREE	Trent Baker

Writer, R Johns
Director, Kat Henry

This project has been assisted by the Australian Government through the Australia Council for the Arts, its funding and advisory body.

WRITER NOTES
CHRONOLOGICAL ACKNOWLEDGEMENTS

To Peta Hanrahan who first saw the potential in this script and took me to Big West under the umbrella of the Dog Theatre. Peta had the inspired idea of presenting the project at the Substation Newport, in the old Workshop.

To Kate Shearer, former artistic Director of Big West who supported the creative development of *Stray*.

To Marcia Ferguson, Artistic Director, Big West Festival for her belief in the project. Big West Festival produced the play in November 2013 at The Substation Newport. To Jeremy Gaden, Director of the Substation, for his generous support throughout all stages of the *Stray* project.

Stray was realised with assistance from the Australian Government through the Australia Council, its arts funding and advisory body, in both its early development and its subsequent showing at the Big West Festival.

To Anne Browning (director) Hayden Spencer, Melodie Reynolds-Diarra and Brett Ludeman for the creative development.

Selene Bateman at Auspicious Arts.

Jessie McGuire at Lort Smith Animal Hospital.

Gianna my accountant at Alan Dredge for taking me to Bark in The Park.

Erin Milne, Cassandra Gray, David Farmer, Paul and the team at the Substation. Volunteers Shelby Versa, Jasmine Stubbs, Cleo Cutcher and Sarah Platts.

To Kat Henry for dramaturgical advice and directorial vision.

To John Shearman who took on the role of Tiga, and for Ngaire Dawn Fair and Trent Baker as the exceptional ensemble of three. To Dan Frederiksen as an actor in rehearsals.

Brett Ludeman for the videography

To Kylie Russell production and stage manager from Big West Festival onwards. Zack Lee for sound design.

Kara Stacey Merrin lighting designer for the creative development and Big West Festival production .

To those who all helped the production—Juliet Bradford, Tim Edhouse, Tim Potter Michael Watson, Daniel Nixon.

To Liz Jones for programming this play at La Mama Courthouse. My appreciation for Liz's long time support of my work.

To all the staff at La Mama who provide invaluable assistance, Maureen Hartley, Caitlin Dullard, Bec Etchell and Nedd Jones, Amber Hart and Mary Helen Sassman.

The current team in this publication—for their dedication, passion and inspiration in making the work. We welcome Linda Hum as lighting designer.

Peter Mumford whose dog Tiga became the inspiration for this play. Peter has been there from the beginning and at all stages of the project as sounding board for the writing and its physical realisation. His design has shaped the journey of the performance. Peter also designed the cover for this Currency Press publication.

To all who have been on the journey of *Stray*, thank you for your support, input and belief.

The central journey of Tiga is both classical and contemporary. Set in an often brutal world, the savagery of the landscape and the vigorously colloquial text and the guilelessness of the protagonist all combine to offer a raw and moving tale, comedic, poignant, resonant and bold: a profound eulogy for the innocent.

ACTORS AND CHARACTERS

This script demands challenging and transformative performances from all its cast members, astute observation, physicality and versatility, so that the actors can find the beating heart of each character, both dog and human. The final rendering is then totally authentic.

TIGA the Doberman is played by ACTOR ONE, who maintains the single character throughout the play. This is because Tiga the dog is the protagonist. The script is from Tiga's perspective. He is the anchor for the piece. Tiga is a sentient being, who dreams, is anxious, brave and bold. He knows what it is to love and what it means to be bullied and coerced. What it means to be abandoned. Whatever trials and torments, tests and disappointment he experiences, he adventures on. As in all epic journeys, his identity holds the key to his future.

Actors TWO and THREE play the multiple characters Tiga encounters on his Homeric journey.

Actors TWO and THREE also play characters who need the dog's help, such as Bones the Butcher, Miss Lentils and Bus Driver. They too have the challenge of embodying dogs: Kelpie, Tiga's Mum, Poodle, Bluey in the rescue home and Killer, the pit bull.

The talking animal is an ancient tradition in storytelling as it carries with it deep truths about the human world. In *Stray*, human nature is seen through the eyes of a dog. He is exposed to the best and worst of humankind.

The idea of the play is to hold up a mirror to human nature and the virtues, (e.g., love, compassion and kindness) and vices (e.g., brutality, exploitation) which emanate from it and which impact on the dog. For example, some of the characters are involved with drugs. These are portrayed as weak individuals with the potential to cause suffering to the protagonist.

The savagery of human nature is shown in the dogfights for human 'entertainment,' helping to raise our awareness of animals as sentient beings.

Animal Rights continue to be an important issue in the twenty-first century.

STYLE

Non naturalistic—two of the actors play fourteen and fifteen characters each—signifying changes and transformations with voice, gesture and physicality, rather than costume and make-up.

Experimental and physical—the performance of the dog is not literal, in the sense that the actor does the entire play on his/her hands and knees. The performance is informed by how humans interpret a dog's behaviour and physicality.

Gestures however minimal or abstract, have to be coded in a way that the audience read and believe 'this is a dog'.

This is Rough Theatre—anarchic, intense and immediate.

The speech of the play is colloquial as well as poetic and the writer has invented what she perceives as suitable dog language.

There are shifting time lines, incorporating memory sequences with Tiga's mum and the dog dream sequences with Kelpie and Poodle.

The play could be described as Epic in style, as Tiga is on a journey of adventure and self-discovery.

The Homeric Odyssey of the dog demands a style that shifts and changes—capturing the moments of brief encounters, the open road, the long or short-term relationships with different owners, the times when Tiga seems settled and the times when he continues his journey into dangerous places and uncertainty.

DESIGN

The set design is minimal as the play is centered on physical performance.

Presenting the play in traverse, as in this La Mama Courthouse production, means the performers are virtually enclosed. The dog's journey is through the suburbs, so the audiences become like the suburbs, surrounding the dog. The set encompasses the physical performances, and is minimal to facilitate the fast transitions of the actors. There can be no interruption to the action. There is no fourth wall. The overall feeling of the design is to encourage the audience to feel part of the action.

The minimal set and props facilitate the multiple character transitions and diverse locations. Actors are creating the environment, not the set design.

Audience members are seated on rostra that are raised above the action, to create the effect of looking down into a dog pit.

VIDEO

The video has a rough documentary quality, and is shot from the P.O.V. (point of view) of the dog. The dog's perspective means low camera angles and monochrome presentation to capture some of the animal's limited colour perception.

LIGHTING

Tiga's mum, Poodle and Kelpie are memory and dream dogs, so there are special lighting states for them.

Note the shadows of the birds under the grille, and the use of torches.

SOUND

The soundscape creates an underlying immersive environment that transports and connects audiences with the immediate setting they are moving into. Tiga travels through more than twenty-three different environments and spaces, exterior and interior. The sound designer wanted to create an atmosphere of innocence trapped in a foreign and unforgiving place, with a combination of electric and acoustic instruments, as well as 'found' sounds. The sound design attempts to evoke something small and beautiful within something harsh and ominous.

COSTUMES

Costumes are minimal, as they need to be easily accessible by the actors and easily dispensed with. No props or costume should retard the action. There is no decorative quality in set/ props/ costume, only what is physically utilised by performers. If it is not used it shouldn't be there.

LANGUAGE

A language has been invented where appropriate, to attempt to convey the dog's perception and experience. For example, words such as Dogbright, Dogdark, Waggingcrazy, Cracklebomb, Bite trap, Lapalap.

Names of characters often arise either from sounds the dog hears e.g., Squeaky, who has a high voice; or from how he hears characters introduced by others, e.g., the pet shop girl abusing one of the customers as a Wanker.

Slouchy is an indicator of body language, for dogs read body language with great acuity. Yet Tiga refers to him as Chickenfed because he can smell the takeaway chicken the character is constantly eating. Bones comes from the smell of meat on the butcher.

Every character has a different voice, capturing class and taste and fashion.

The hipsters use words like 'totes, amazeballs, pop-up', whereas the fighting dog Killer has a truncated language formed around the fighting ring. His words are violent and shaped by the broken and battered bodies of the dogs in the ring.

Tiga's voice on his solo journey is poetic, close to stream of consciousness. It is a quality and form similar to the beat poets—short sentences, capturing the world through perception. These poets were also famous for their travels on the road. The monologues allow the dog to describe the world using his interior voice.

CHARACTERS

ACTOR ONE	TIGA
ACTOR TWO	MRS GOLDFISH / PET SHOP GIRL/ JANELLE/ TIGA'S MUM/ SQUEAKY/ RGW/ KELPIE/ SKINNY/ /HANNAH / TOPSY/ MISS LENTILS / CASEY / GRUFF GIRL / POLICE ONE / SPONGE WOMAN
ACTOR THREE	MR GOLDFISH / MR HAPPY SMELLS / BOY / WANKER / POODLE / KILLER / TOBY / BONES THE BUTCHER / ALFONSO / SLOUCHY / BUS DRIVER / POLICE TWO / BLUE HEELER / MALE VET

SETTING

The play is about a Homeric journey of a dog. He travels through multiple locations, homes, streets, parks and backyards of the city. I have named Melbourne suburbs in this script. However in any place this play is performed those suburbs can be changed. In every city there is a fractured heart, a social divide and character types whom a dog is likely to meet on his wanderings.

The last Doberman in a pet shop, in a shopping centre, in Altona. He is curled up; fast asleep on the floor. He stirs scratching his ears and his belly. He opens his eyes.

TIGA: Whoah! This is waggingcrazy! You looking at me and me looking at you! [*Direct address to audience*] Hello, I'm Westie number nine. Next to me is mad Kelpie and over there is the poopy Poodle, all of us at Pets-To-Go. If you want a best friend I can go home with you right now. I will be your best, bestest friend forever and when you're in the sad-dogs like I sometimes am because my Mum's gone I don't know where, I can tumble for you! [*Running the words together*] My 'lookmumIcantumble'. [*He somersaults, jumps up, clapping his hands*] Hey! Who wants licketylicks? Take me! Take me! Take me!

Little barks as he jumps up and down.

MR GOLDFISH: The kids'll love him.

MRS GOLDFISH: [*pouting*] Aren't Dobermans aggressive? We want a nice dog.

TIGA: All pouty fish lips. Like the fancy goldfish opposite. It's a human goldfish.

MRS GOLDFISH: I want a poodle, love. They're civilized. Poodles sit in the back of the car and look out the window like people interested in shops and scenery.

MR GOLDFISH: I thought a doggy dog might be fun for the kids.

MRS GOLDFISH: But the kids need to be set an example. Poodles sit on the chairs in the lounge and look at you like a person wanting to have a conversation.

MR GOLDFISH: There's a poodle over there. Lovely curly hair.

MRS GOLDFISH: Lovely. That's what I want—lovely curly hair that won't shed and malt all over the carpets. It's a nice tidy dog for a nice tidy house.

TIGA: Don't go! I can make you happy human goldfish! Come back! NO [*Becoming a howl*] NOOO!

PET SHOP GIRL: Christmas is over now. If you want to be sold you have to be cute. See over there. The lift comes up here. The human peeps come outta there and they only buy smiley puppies. And if no-one buys you it's off to the pound with you. You're a runt.

TIGA: What's a runt? What's a pound?

MR HAPPY SMELLS: [*with a Russian accent*] What I want... [*High, farting sound*] That's better... never hold wind in, is bad for intestines.

TIGA: [*excitedly*] So good!

MR HAPPY SMELLS: ...Is bomb sniffer dog. Can this one sniff bombs?

TIGA: [*sniffing the air*] Wagging crazy. Real nice. Like to have a roll in that. Whoah! [*Delightedly*] Cracklebomb again, Mr Happy Smells!

PET SHOP GIRL: There's no bombs out this way sir so I don't know. Are you in customs?

MR HAPPY SMELLS: Nyet. Security. What's his security credentials?

PET SHOP GIRL: He's a pup.

MR HAPPY SMELLS: Were his mum and dad attack dogs?

PET SHOP GIRL: I dunno maybe.

MR HAPPY SMELLS: [*farting sounds*] There we go again... sauerkraut in soup causes flatulence. Is form of psychological warfare.

TIGA: Ripper! [*Madly wagging*] Another cracklebomb. This is so exciting.

MR HAPPY SMELLS: I'm expert.

TIGA: I'm piddling.

MR HAPPY SMELLS: He's no better than girl. Girls want to wee all the time. Weak bladders. Show me the Kelpie. I want dog with good set of teeth and balls. Kelpie is that kind of dog.

TIGA: Press my nose up against the glass. Maybe my mum'll come out the door that opens and closes with all the people pouring out. A smiley face presses on the glass next to mine.

Lighting change.

BOY: Can I have that dog with the floppy ears?

JANELLE: [*vocalising on one breath and at speed*] You've had your presents you wanted a kitten and because you weren't looking after it your father reversed over it and I had to clean it up all that mashed cat over the concrete you're never having an animal for Christmas again.

TIGA: Take me! Take me! I want to be your Christmas present.

BOY *and* TIGA *mirror each other jumping up and down.*

BOY: Give me money for that dog!

JANELLE: No! Too excitable we'd have to chain him up and what if he runs in circles all day and chokes himself because you're not outside because you don't know how to look after anything and I'd be the one walking and feeding it and having to deal with the neighbours complaining that it's barking because its bored out of its mind while you're playing your really expensive video games.

TIGA: Take Me! Me! Me!

BOY: I wish, I wish for that dog.

JANELLE: Yuk look at him slobbering that dog'll bite he will he'll be a savage when he's bigger then we'd have to put him down.

BOY: What's put him down?

JANELLE: He goes to sleep forever.

BOY: I still want him, to play with.

JANELLE *pulls screaming* BOY *away.*

JANELLE: Shut up.

Lighting change. WANKER *enters. He kneels and clicks his fingers coaxing the pup.*

TIGA: Another peep in front of me. Sniff it. Smoke smell clinging to my fur.

PET SHOP GIRL: Fucking wanker…

TIGA: [*dreamily*] Wanker. … [*To audience*] What's a fucking wanker?

PET SHOP GIRL: [*to* WANKER *who has the last of a rolled up ciggie*] This is a smoke free zone, you wanker.

TIGA: The Wanker looks at me all alone in my glass box.

TIGA *rolling on his back.*

Please take me. I don't want to get sent away.
Wanker's tickling my tummy. Ha ha ha!

WANKER: Hello waggers. You're a little cutie.

TIGA: I'll love you forever and ever… I've never felt this before. My eyes are getting bigger and bigger. And the rest of me is getting smaller and smaller.

WANKER: How much?

PET SHOP GIRL: Nine hundred.

Fast bidding starts.

WANKER: I'll give you five hundred.
TIGA: He'll give you five hundred.
PET SHOP GIRL: Would you give me eight eighty?
TIGA: Can you go to eight eighty?
WANKER: Five thirty.
TIGA: Five thirty.
PETGIRL: I need eight seventy.
TIGA: She needs eight seventy.
WANKER: Five fifty.
TIGA: She can't do five fifty. He can't do eight seventy. What'll we do?
PET SHOP GIRL: We'll call the breeder on such a low bid.
TIGA: C'mon, give her the money! I love you.
WANKER: Six hundred.
TIGA: Sticks hundred! Sticks hundred! We've got sticks hundred now!
PETGIRL: Last offer eight forty.

    WANKER *exits, shaking his head.*

Fucking wanker!
TIGA: Wanker!
    NOOOO!
    You're going in the wrong direction you Wanker!!!
    Oh no!!!! NOOO!
[*Whimpering*]. Don't go. Don't walk away. He doesn't look back. My nose is all snuffly. I put it between my paws.
    Pet Girl closes the shop. Dogdark now. Time to sleep.
    The poopy Poodle got sold, even the mad Kelpie. What's wrong with me?
    No sale!
    Silence.

Mum please come up the lift door that opens and closes, opens and closes.
    Come an' take me home. All the other pups were stuffing their faces on her titties and I could never get a look in. I count titties one, two, three, four, five, sticks, seven, eight. Where's my tittie mum?

    Lighting change night. TIGA*'s* MUM *appears in his memory.*

TIGA'S MUM: Westie number nine. You'll have to be a thinker not a teat sucker.

If you want to have a happy life, chase a tennis ball in the day, catch a seagull on the wing. Count rabbits at night.

Some of your relatives are schweinen hunden tear the throats out of anyone. We're big prick dogs. Except you, Westie. The last one out of nine. The littlest.

You'll have to make something of yourself in other ways.

That's what Westie's do, they never give in against the odds.

Remember you were born by the Altona tanks, the flames dancing in the sky; there was the shriek of the trains and the salt of the sea breeze.

It's a special place and it makes you special.

Remember wherever you go, no-one can beat you down. Tell them to shut their bite trap.

And when you are sad talk to old great grandfather in the moon. He's a magic fella.

TIGA *and* TIGA'S MUM *howl.*

TIGA: And I'd fall asleep curled up next to her belly.

Licking the little drops of milk that came my way…

Lighting change to pet shop daytime.

The smells wake me up. Oh my, oh my, oh my, it's Wanker. He's back.

Ohmyohmyohmy. I'm piddling. Streams of piddle. I'm so happy.
WANKER: I've got six twenty.
TIGA: He's got sticks twenty.
PET SHOP GIRL: Would you give me fifty more?
WANKER: Take it or leave it.
PET SHOP GIRL: If you're that poor how you'll feed him?
TIGA: Good point.
WANKER: One day I'll be rich. I'm studying climate science.
PET SHOP GIRL: Oh yeah, so what's the weather forecast?
WANKER: Raining cheap dogs.
PET SHOP GIRL: You wish.
TIGA: I can do more piddle. Piddle here. Piddle there.
WANKER: I'll give you six forty, six fifty.

TIGA: Sticks fifty, sticks fifty!!! We got sticks fifty.
WANKER: Six fifty or I'll walk.
PET SHOP GIRL: Nah. It's much more with papers.
WANKER: It's the dog I want. Not the papers.
TIGA: Going, going—
PET SHOP GIRL: Done.
TIGA: I'm sold. Wonderful Wanker is mine!

> *Lighting change.* TIGA*'s new home is a rented house in Altona. Darkness.* WANKER *and* SQUEAKY *with torches.*

SQUEAKY: Welcome to Altona! How could they rent out a house with a smashed window?
TIGA: New smells.
SQUEAKY: Was it a burglary?
TIGA: It's another hand. All soft, another peep. A squeaky one.
SQUEAKY: Or domestic violence!
WANKER: You're always imagining.
SQUEAKY: It feels so spooky.
TIGA: The energy is scary but don't be scaredy cats. I wag my tail. When peeps are scared you have to protect them. Wagging really hard.
SQUEAKY: He's good luck.
TIGA: It's so good to be here.
SQUEAKY: Look how happy he is. Happy dog.
WANKER: He's a pedigree. I told Pets-To-Go I didn't want the papers but what's to say they even had them.
SQUEAKY: Do we care?
TIGA: No.
WANKER: No but there's something suss.
SQUEAKY: Like what?
WANKER: Not sure. Shady breeder. If they're pedigree Dobermans can get floppy neck.
SQUEAKY: So it's good if he's not a pedigree.
WANKER: Ten years and the neck goes would be awful.
SQUEAKY: Now who's imagining. He'll be fine.
TIGA: I love it here because I'm with you.
SQUEAKY: He's soooo adorable!!!!!! Oh he's so cute! [*Tickling* TIGA] Look at his flopsywopsy bunnykin bits.

TIGA: [*small, snapping sound as he clings to* WANKER] I belong to him.
SQUEAKY: Oh babe he's so sweet. Where will he sleep? [*Patting next to her*] How about just here on the bed!

> TIGA *rushes over to sit beside her.*

WANKER: NOT on the bed! NO! Look at his paws he's going to be huge. [*holding* TIGA*'s paws over* SQUEAKY*'s head*] Let me put him there… in his own bed over here.

> TIGA *is placed in the opposite corner.*

SQUEAKY: So perfect!
TIGA: Sounds like cat PURRFECT. Chase your feet.

> WANKER *and* SQUEAKY *have their arms around each other as they sleep.*

They lie in bed I watch 'em closely.
> Wanker on his back does big snores. Squeaky squeaks.
> This is my job. Guarding the snore squeaks.
> I need to do a big poo now. It's a nice carpet. Grey … soft.

> TIGA *slides on his backside all the way across the floor, with great enjoyment.*

Oh yeah! Yeah. Oh yeah!
WANKER: [*waking up*] What's that disgusting smell? [*Jumping up*] Oh fuck.
TIGA: Uh oh.
WANKER: I'm going to throw up.
TIGA: Its only Pets-To-Go pellets. Mixed with last night's mince.
WANKER: I'm taking him back now.
TIGA: Don't.
SQUEAKY: It's Sunday, they're closed.
WANKER: It's everywhere.
TIGA: He's so not happy.
SQUEAKY: He doesn't know. Do you poppet?

> *Snap of lighting change.* TIGA, WANKER *and* SQUEAKY *in the sunny outside.*

TIGA: Out into the dogbright! Into the long grass. A hand presses my bum down. She seems to want to see me poo again.

WANKER *and* SQUEAKY *watch* TIGA *intently*.

How odd. I've just done a big shit all over the bedroom and now she wants another round. This is really hard there's nothing left. I do my best. Aagh! A tiny little bit plops out.

SQUEAKY: Good boy. Here's a biscuit.

TIGA: Wanker's got a big smile on his face now.

WANKER: Yeah good boy.

TIGA: So you want to watch me poo in the grass?
Is that right?

WANKER *and* SQUEAKY: [*with delight*] YES!

TIGA: I'll do my very best to only ever go outside in the grass.

[*To audience member*] I do feel a bit sensitive if people watch me poo because well truth be told it's a little odd all this excitement!

[*To* WANKER *and* SQUEAKY] But I've got it! As Mum said, 'Your job is to serve.'

[*Bouncing up and down*] I feel so much lighter. So excited! I came good! [*Action of shovelling dirt over the poo*] Why am I bounding?

I'm a bit unco. My big paws are all tangled up, get in the way. Run smack into the wall.

WANKER: He's so funny!

SQUEAKY: He's so bouncy. He's like Tigger in *Winnie the Pooh*!

TIGA: My Mum said that. Keep bouncing.

WANKER: What's that Tiga? You like that name?

TIGA: It's a name with balls of steel!

WANKER: Yeah!

WANKER *and* SQUEAKY *exit*.

Lighting change and soundscape. TIGA *in the garden.*

TIGA: Home alone.
Chew on my tennis ball.
Don't stare at the gate too much when he leaves in the car.
When's he coming back?
What to do now?
Relax, chill out under the tree, feel the sun on my face.
No way.

I've got a job to do.
Guard the place from dangerous intruders.
Myna birds! An army of them. Invading,
Squawking on the grass.
Cocky arrogant strut-abouts.
Hunt them down.
Focus with every fibre of my being.
Muscles twitching, tense.
Pretend I'm not there
As their chatter fills the air.
Advance slowly hackles up
Stalk and shiver, drool and stare.
Front paw raised.
Ready to pounce,
Eucalypt cracks as I leap.
Birds fly away in a beat.
Not even a tail feather between my teeth.
Toss my ratty basketball after them
Get gone you rogues and don't come back.
Drag my fake grass bed under the old gum tree.
Not too close to humming, honeysuckle fence
Angry fellas clinging there. Let them be.
Send my voice out loud.
Yeah that's good.
Everyone in the neighbourhood can hear me.
WHERE ARE YOU? I'M ALL ALONE.
But please don't stress.
I'm looking after everything, doing my best.
The wind blows through the gutters… fight the wind… gottcha…
Postie… Flip out… that banging letter box… [*Big deep barking*]
Pee against the spiky soft needle bush.
GOOOO the dumb kids tearing up the picket fence bit by bit.
I go sniffing.
What's that?
Something in the back yard.

Tea bags [*Looking under audience chairs.*] Nope. Onion bits nope. Yep! A corncob.

So good. So nice. [*Rolling it around.*] Swallow it.

Soundscape fades, lighting change as TIGA *on all fours attempts to throw up.*

It's inside my neck.
Get it out!
Claw it out.
Where's the vacuum hose suck it out.
Corncob! Corncob! Call 000!
I hate this corncob.
Hard to breathe.

WANKER *rushes in.*

WANKER: What's the matter?
TIGA: Corncob.
WANKER: Please don't die Tiga.
TIGA: I got corncob in my throat.
WANKER: We'll take you to Lort Smith.
TIGA: Save me! Save me!
WANKER: You have to save him!

Lights change to Lort Smith Animal Hospital. A VET *puts on rubber gloves, she is* RGW: *Rubber-Gloved Woman.* WANKER *and* RGW *at either side of* TIGA.

TIGA: Awful sharp clean smell.
RGW: What seems to be the problem?
WANKER: He was choking before; I don't know what's wrong with him.
TIGA: It's a corncob.
RGW: Look away from the needle now. It's dislodged. But now it's stuck in your intestine. We'll have to slit the belly. We'll make you better; you're just going to sleep. It won't hurt. Keep still now.
TIGA: Wag my tail. Show willing. A big shiny pointed jab, then another jab through me. Don't make a sound. Mum said big prick dogs never cry. Have to be strong for peeps an' Wwwaaannk… ahhhhh…
Ten, nine, eight, seven…
RGW: How about we neuter him at the same time too?
TIGA: Hey?
RGW: It would be prudent.

TIGA: Waas noota prooden?

> *Lighting change. Soundscape.* TIGA *dreams whilst under anaesthesia. He lies on his back as his four limbs move in slow motion.* POODLE *and* KELPIE, *who were in the pet shop with* TIGA, *enter together.* POODLE *is refined,* KELPIE *is excitable and energetic.*

What are Poodle and Kelpie doing in my dream?
POODLE: I may have been born with curly hair but I am clever-clever. [*To audience member*] Pat me! Pat me! I am totally gorgeous.
KELPIE: What we gorging on? What's the tucker? Tucker?
POODLE: Balls, Prick Ears.
KELPIE: I'm slobbering already.
POODLE: We are eating them as appetizers at the après-ski ball. We dance first then eat.
KELPIE: Are the sheep coming? Do you want me to round them up? Round 'em up?
TIGA: Can I come?
KELPIE: Not any more drongo!
POODLE: The undesired consequence of a rowdy rooting Doberman gatecrashing the après-ski ball is ghastly. So safeguards have been put in place. All invited guests are Sheep.
KELPIE: I'll pen the sheep and we'll gobble up the spermy, slobby balls.
POODLE: We poach them Prick Ears in redcurrant juice.
KELPIE: Bloody and rare 'll do. Bloody and rare.

> POODLE *and* KELPIE *exit into the shadows.*

TIGA: I can smell them already.

> *Lighting snap change.*

> *As* TIGA *comes too,* WANKER *and* RGW *are looking down at him from either side.*

WANKER: How is he? Will he be all right?
TIGA: Yes! I came good.
RGW: Could have been touch and go.
But he's a battler and he's hung in there. See he's doing really well. He's quite alert.
TIGA: Look at my stitches!

RGW: It'll be a scar for life.
TIGA: Check out the scar… All he way down to my… shit… where's my balls gone?
    Never go to sleep again I might lose something else! My ears, my nose…
    WHAT'S HAPPENED TO MY BALLS?
RGW: He'll still be happy smelling the girls wee. But he won't be able to…
TIGA: [*underscoring*] Oh no.
RGW: It was a wise decision to have him neutered. Some men feel if the dog is neutered it reflects on them…
TIGA: Them! Them! Them! What about me? My rooting hours have just been wiped out.
RGW: So many unwanted pups are dumped or drowned.
TIGA: What about all the hot bitches who might want me?
RGW: And it would be prudent to microchip him.
WANKER: Woah! Woah!
RGW: Another wise decision.
TIGA: WHAT! My balls are gone! What'll microchip do?
WANKER: What made him sick?
TIGA: I told you it was a corncob.

    Lighting change. TIGA *is back home in Altona.*

[*To audience*] And Wanker takes corncob and hangs it in the house. But that evil corncob is laughing at me. And it's just out of my reach.

    [*Jumping*] Even when I jump real high. That corncob is just dying to see me get wiped out.

    WANKER *enters with long lead.*

WANKER: Walk.
TIGA: [*pushing* WANKER] WALK!!!!! Shutup!!! WALK. Run ten times around the kitchen non-stop.
WANKER: Calm down. You know the routine. Choke collar on with lead.

    WANKER *attaches the rope lead to* TIGA*'s collar. Lighting change as they go for their walk.*

TIGA: Out the door, down the path, dragging that poor Wanker behind me.
WANKER: DON'T PULL!
TIGA: HURRY UP!!!
WANKER: Stop pulling. I can't keep up! STOP IT. Or we go the other way.
    TURN AROUND.

    WANKER gets tangled up in the lead.

TIGA: Where are you going?
WANKER: Now are you going to behave?
TIGA: You need to practice. Speed up.
WANKER: Don't rush me.
TIGA: You're getting all wound up.
WANKER: Focus.
TIGA: Where's my treats for behaving?
WANKER: Sit.
TIGA: Give me my liver treat!!!
WANKER: Sit down!
TIGA: NOW.
WANKER: Not on my foot!!!!!!
    Calm down.
    SIT. Good boy.
    Paw.
TIGA: Give me my ball.
WANKER: Give me your paw.
TIGA: BALL!
WANKER: Other paw.
TIGA: Let me off the lead.
WANKER: BALL. FETCH!
TIGA: Away we go. [*Runs off, then realising* WANKER *is teasing him with a fake ball throw, growls advancing on* WANKER. *Ball is thrown and* TIGA *chases it.*] Away we go!
WANKER: Bring it back! Here!
TIGA: Don't want you to have it. Mine!
WANKER: DROP IT! DROP IT!
TIGA: All slobby and smelly in my mouth.

WANKER gets the ball from TIGA and throws it far away.

WANKER: Sniff! Find! Go!

Lighting change. Soundscape. TIGA *hurls himself after the ball.*

TIGA: SPLAASH.
Into the muddy reedy water
Snakes slithering away hissing startled.
Paddle past the rusting hulk of shopping trolley water gurgling.
Flight of moorhens, rising up, beating wings cluck cluck.
Muddy slime all over my nose.
Paddle fast, water clinging.
Out the reeds the other side.
DUCK POO! Roll in duck poo. So good! Soft and squishy
Drop the ball.
Maggoty toad smeared on grass
YUM! Lick. Swallow.

WANKER: [*calling*] Tiga.

TIGA: Where's my ball?
Dragon fly whirring wings. Catch it. Snap!
Where's my ball?
Found you!!!
Past the magpies, peck my head.
Catch me if you can you lunatics
And in the faint distance I hear Wanker calling

WANKER: Tiga! Tiga! Come back!

TIGA: Running in bounds. Loping strides.
Gum tree flowers sweet and heady.
Over the sand hillocks …
Sun shadows glass glinting …
Burning. Bad.
Sharp teeth of bottle.
Cuts my front pad.
Slices.
Stops me short.
But I've sniffed them out!

Lighting change, soundscape slow fade out.

TIGA *meets* SKINNY THE DOGMAN *and his fighting dog* KILLER *on a road by the creek.* KILLER *is demented. He has dead eyes that roll around and around in his head.*

SKINNY *throws a chop on the ground near* TIGA.

SKINNY: [*grabbing* KILLER *by the collar, almost choking him, as his tongue hangs out*] Killer!

KILLER: [*to* TIGA] Take your eyes off that chop. Mine! Bite yer. GERROFF!

SKINNY: [*to* TIGA] You'se hungry?

KILLER: Dog bait.

SKINNY: You're good lookin' matie.

KILLER: Dogman mine.

SKINNY: Spit out that that ball! Drop!

TIGA: Uhah.

SKINNY: Want to eat tasty chop-chop? All nice and crunchy. Red with blood.

TIGA: Ahah!

KILLER: Go the Dogbait. Tear him.

SKINNY: Killer's all choked up. Killer won't hurt you. Dogman's here. I'll give you a good feed. That's it. Get in matie. Get in the back of the van.

TIGA: Stomach rules. Scramble up into the dark blood smell of van.

KILLER: Bite. Trap.

KILLER *and* SKINNY *trap* TIGA.

SKINNY: Stay there you maggot.

TIGA: Wanker won't know where I am. Grrrr. If I had balls I'd go spotface Dogman.

KILLER: You bite Dogman. I'll kill you.

SKINNY: You're stubborn as—

TIGA: Don't understand.
Have to find my ball.
Get back to Wanker.
Lighting change.

SKINNY: The North's your new home matie!

> TIGA *in the yard at* SKINNY THE DOGMAN's *place.* KILLER *attempts to attack* TIGA.

KILLER: Dogbait! Raw meat! Tear your face off dogbait.
TIGA: What's wrong with you?
KILLER: Dogman mine.
TIGA: I know!
KILLER: Win, win, win. Kill dogbait. Win, win, win.
TIGA: Why am I here?
KILLER: Gamester. Bet.
TIGA: What is that?
KILLER: Gamesters yell. Paper money. Holler. Ding bell. Dogman calls. Bite. Fight. Kill.
TIGA: When?
KILLER: Chop comes. Killer takes Bloody chunks from face. All the dogbaits. Stiff. No dogbaits live.
TIGA: Yeah but when?
KILLER: Clump, clump, clump. Gamesters come.
TIGA: Run away. Don't fight.
KILLER: Dogman hit you four by two dogbait. Thwack, thwack.
TIGA: Why?
KILLER: It's what Dogmen do. Do or die.

> *Lighting snap change.* SKINNY *creeps up behind* TIGA. *He slips a chop on a string around* TIGA's *neck.* KILLER *and* TIGA *face each other in the dog-fighting ring.*

TIGA: What's going on? Why've I got the meaty chop?
SKINNY: You'll be chops soon.
KILLER: Feed. Me. Me. Want chop. Blood.
SKINNY: [*calling loudly to audience*] Gamesters. Bets on.
  Go Killer!
  Don't quit till that maggot dogbait is torn to pieces! Bite! Fight! Kill!
KILLER: Brain dead Killer charges. Leaps up.
TIGA: Hot breath on my face.
  Don't Killer! Stop!
SKINNY: Gamesters shout. Fight! Fight! Fight!
TIGA: Run away fast… Skinny hits me hard.

KILLER: Thwack! Thwack! Thwack! Thwack!
    Killer leaps.
TIGA: I leap.
SKINNY: Forelegs lock. Claw.
TIGA: But I'm bigger go the neck real hard. Sink my teeth…
KILLER: Hairless skin.
TIGA: Blood in my mouth.
KILLER: Hot breath.
TIGA: Under my ribs snapping at my scar.
KILLER: Stab of pain.
SKINNY: Leap again.
TIGA: Die for Dogman?
    Die for Killer?
    Shut their bite traps.
    Wanker's waiting for me.
    I snap.
KILLER: Bone sticks out of Killer.
SKINNY: Yellow bone through fur.
TIGA: I stick my claws in his swollen eyes.
SKINNY: Blood pours.

    KILLER *howls.*

  Rip to pieces.
TIGA: Go the throat.
    Shake and toss.
TIGA, SKINNY *and* KILLER: Thump. Thump. Thump. Thump. Thump. Thump.

    KILLER *on the ground,* TIGA *has his head.*

TIGA: Thump, thump, thump, thump against the post.
    Skull splits.
    Brains burst.
    Blood.
SKINNY: GER OFF YOU MAGGOT!
TIGA: Trembling bad.
    Wobbily knees.
    Exhausted.
    I've got smell of Killer's blood on me.

Lighting change as SKINNY *stands in the ring shocked at seeing* KILLER's *lifeless body.*

SKINNY: Fuck me dog's dead. [*Turning sharply holding mobile phone to ear as it rings. He talks into the phone*] Stuff's ready to come in... Yeah... bit choked up at the moment, someone in me family just died... loved Killer me pittie better than me Mum and Dad... it's killin' me... don't talk about it, it's doing me head in... you like dogs matie? Yeah? Want a dog? This dog protects shit and it'd look awesome on a lead walking down Chapel St. It'll be a chick magnet [*Aiming a vicious kick at* TIGA *who yelps*] You do? It's a pedigree. So it's 2 Gs. I'll sell him cheap he's missing his best mate Killer. Gotta go. Can't talk no more. Cut up so bad.

He ends the phonecall.

Got some money for you maggot. Big money.

Skinny ain't stupid. Money Rules.

Slow fade as lights change. TIGA *at home in Abbotsford with* TOBY *his new owner. Soundscape. Night.* TOBY *and* TIGA *have raybans on.* TOBY *is smoking a joint.*

TOBY: Yeah. This is relaxing bro. Meth was making me paranoid.

TIGA: No more scratchy scratches skinscratch days.

TOBY: Yeah. This weed is amazeballs.

TIGA *starts to circle at speed chasing his tail.*

TIGA: This is amazeballs bro! You want happy? Here's how! Nose goes to bottom. Bottom goes to nose! Jolly bottoms full of smiley smells.

TOBY: [*laughing*] You want a toke? Watch me! Watch me! Watch me! Now you.

TIGA *sneezes violently as* TOBY *blows the smoke in his face.*

Oh bro how random, a sneeze catching you by surprise, like a meth lab going sky-high. Skinny used too much paint stripper cooking the meth. That was his downfall bro. Crystal falling from the sky onto his spotty charface. Sky fall! Hey we're Bond! [*Taking off a James Bond voice*] James Bond. Shaken not stirred.

TIGA: Who's Bond Bro?

TOBY: Bond bro. I 've got the munchies. Retro Rice Bubbles?

TIGA: Yeah! Go the Rice Bubbles box. Fight it. Toss it. Hey my head's stuck! I don't know if I'm going to live or die!
TOBY: Oh my God, I knew it! You can even reference Bond Movies!
TIGA: [*muffled in the cereal box*] Did I?
TOBY: [*lying on floor playing air guitar*] You know you did, you know you did, you know you did.
TIGA: I'm trapped. Can't get the box off. Hey you out there. I can't see.
TOBY: I'm going to piss myself! Live and Let die.
TIGA: Yeah I'm piddling! Ohmyohmyohmy. Live and let die.

> TIGA *finds a way to get his head out of the cereal box. At the same time,* HANNAH *who has returned from Berlin stands at the entrance, finger to doorbell. Lights and sound change.*

HANNAH: Dingen Dongen.
TOBY: Holy shit! Is that Hannah? Got to calm down. Calm down bro. Take deep breaths.
  No more tearing shit.
TIGA: Exterminate! Exterminate! Exterminate!
TOBY: Do my eyes look too red? How do I get up?
TIGA: C'mon! Legs go!
TOBY: Hannah's meant to be in Berlin.
TIGA: [*deep barking*] RRRUNNN to the door. What's happened to your legs?

> HANNAH *enters. She throws German words herr, bitte, into the dialogue.*

HANNAH: Guten Abend Herr Toby! Didn't you hear me ring the bell?
TOBY: Hannah! Lovely Hannah.
HANNAH: I knew to keep the key. Can't you get up?
TOBY: Look who else is here!
HANNAH: What the…! Get off me.
TIGA: Hey there!
HANNAH: Get down! Are you pet sitting?
TIGA: I live here.
TOBY: How was Berlin?
HANNAH: Whose dog is it?
TOBY: He's kind of moved in.

HANNAH: What do you mean, Toby? You are not seriously telling me this is permanent.
TOBY: Would that not be good?
TIGA: To be here for good?
HANNAH: Nein. Nein. Nein.
TOBY: You're jetlagged.
HANNAH: I wish I'd stayed in Berlin. They begged me. Madchen bitte bitte.
TIGA: Cheer up. We can do that here. Bitey bitey.
HANNAH: He's mad.
TOBY: Don't be like that.
HANNAH: Like what.
TOBY: He's feeling insecure don't judge him. [*Whispering so* TIGA *can't hear*] He was living in horrible conditions over the Western ring road. Third world. Out where we get the meth and the hydroponic. I took him on.
HANNAH: You what!!!!!!!
TOBY: I saved him.
TIGA: [*mounting her leg*] You need a latte. How about we all go out for lattes?
HANNAH: Will you get off my legs you STUPID QUADRUPED.
TIGA: So high decibel. Tell her to stop PIERCING my ears.
TOBY: Calm down.
HANNAH: How could you make a stupid lifelong mistake and burden us with this!
TOBY: It's not a mistake. He was guarding the crystal. Then he inspired me to give up crystal and grow dope and I'm not being ripped of with the hydroponics.
HANNAH: I don't want a drug patch.
TOBY: What?
HANNAH: Sprechen sie Englisch? I want a real garden, with kale, spinach, sunflowers, corn—
TIGA: What did she say? Corn? Did she say CORN? NO CORN.
TOBY: You hungry Bond?
TIGA: How about some of that gluten-free lactose-free soy bacon bro?
TOBY: Lets see if there's any Cheurizo paprika flavoured sausage left.
HANNAH: Will you stop talking to the dog? I'm here.

TOBY: What's with the tone?

TIGA: [*hiding*] Uh oh fight!

HANNAH: You are reminding me of my Dad. And that makes me really emotional because he was so selfish. He got free education, low-cost housing and didn't make the world better for us. He just got high. Is that all you want in life Toby? To get high so greed and global warming is all our kids have to look forward to?

TOBY: We don't have kids.

HANNAH: Dad forgot what he believed in, took so many drugs he turned into a zombie. Drugs are the way the CIA and the Illuminati control us. Berlin is where it's at. Not mashed up brains from drugs. Urban agriculture. Beekeeping on top of buildings. Moss graffiti. We mix it, pulverize it with yoghurt, spray it with water and see it grow.

TOBY: I could keep him outside.

TIGA: [*poking his head out of his hiding place*] I can make myself really small and fit in.

HANNAH: Six months ago when I left you, you were heartbroken, you cried... don't go, come back.

TIGA: [*remembering*] Like Wanker. How could I have forgotten Wanker?

HANNAH: And all that time I wanted to come back to you.

TIGA: I wanted to go back to him.

HANNAH: I had to fight my desire to stay in Berlin because I wanted to see you.

TIGA: WANKAAH! WAANKKAAH!

TOBY: Everyone's getting upset. Let's have time out. [*To* TIGA] I love you. [*To* HANNAH] And you.

HANNAH: It should just be us.

TIGA: Like Wanker and me before.

TOBY: Then you went away and he became my buddy.

TIGA: I went away and you became my new best friend.

HANNAH: You and the dog or you and me.

TIGA: [*hanging on to* TOBY*'s knee*] You and me. You and me.

TOBY: Yes.

HANNAH: What does that mean?

TIGA: Can I have a pat? A dog biscuit? I'm starting to feel insecure.

HANNAH: He will always be in the way. A dog is so high maintenance.

In Berlin they keep snakes as pets.

> TOBY *has his hand firmly on* TIGA's *collar.*

TOBY: You can't walk snakes.

HANNAH: Snakes have specially designed leads. They can be exercised in the parks. And you know why the Berliners love them?

> *She beckons* TOBY *toward her with sinuous arm movements like a snake charmer,* TOBY *drags* TIGA *behind him as he goes to her.*

Snakes lighten their spirits as genuine,
    Meaningful whimsical pets.
    If we took a cobra for a latte
    It would break people's minds.

TOBY: Amazeballs.

> TOBY *throws* TIGA *in front of him. Now* TIGA, HANNAH *and* TOBY *are in a car.* HANNAH *driving,* TOBY *scrunched up,* TIGA *sits behind them. Night. Soundscape and lighting create the interior of the car.*

Talk to me. He's not talking. Why's he so quiet?

TIGA: You're dumping me.

HANNAH: Stop anthropomorphising. Dogs don't talk. Dogs once lived in the wild. We're setting him free.

TOBY: He just meant a lot to me. Didn't you Bond?

HANNAH: If you miss him get a tattoo of his tail.

TOBY: Why isn't he saying anything? He knows. I feel awful.

HANNAH: I'm not going to apologise to a dog.

TOBY: Tell him to go now.

> TIGA *howls.*

HANNAH: Turn up Bon Iver.

TOBY: Tell him not to follow us home.

HANNAH: Just open the car door and do this in a feel good way.

TOBY: I'm staying in the car.

HANNAH: All right then. I'll do it.

> TOBY *turns up the music, to drown out* TIGA's *howls.*

TIGA: Don't dump me.

HANNAH: Off you go! You're on the other side of the river. Good luck.

Kicks dog out of the car. TIGA *tumbles out yelping.*

TOBY: What was that?
HANNAH: Nothing.
TOBY: Not the dog?
HANNAH: No.

There is silence for a moment as HANNAH *drives on.*

TOBY: Have you heard about Tarquin?
HANNAH: No.
TOBY: He has a pop up café in a café.
HANNAH: No way.
TOBY: Do we want to go for a latte?
HANNAH: Totes babe.

Sound down, lights change. TIGA *has been abandoned on open ground near the river.*

TIGA: I'm meant to be man's best friend. All that cat-crap you told me Mum.

Lighting state for memory as TIGA'S MUM *appears.*

TIGA'S MUM: Serve them no matter how hard they treat you. It's your job to protect them. Otherwise you're no better than a cat son.
TIGA: Oh yeah? Well I want to be a cat.
TIGA'S MUM: Crawl out look at the stars. There's a magic fella up there. See the paw prints in the moon. He ain't a dog and he ain't a cat. Can stand on his hind legs long time, like a man. He taught men how to laugh and how to play.

… Come here pups… Humans have made a picture of the magic fellas on bottles… Our owner loves these bottles. It's why he lies on his backside singing away and drinking it like milk. Study these bottles long and hard so we all can remember how powerful and strong the tigers were when they walked this land. Now magic fella and his missus are looking at us. What do they tell us?

Cascade.

TIGA: Cascade… Pouring a whole lot of love out and that's what we Dobies do better than any other dog.
TIGA'S MUM: So you look up there and ask tigers help when you need it…

> *Lights down on* TIGA'S MUM.

TIGA: I need your help… please help me… please… I'm homeless. I have nowhere to go.

> TOPSY *the cat enters from the tunnel entrance, with a yowl and a hiss.* TIGA *takes a startled step back.*

TOPSY: Hey Dog what's your name?

TIGA: Westie number nine, no better than a girl, runt, waggers, little cutie, Tiga, good boy, matie, maggot, dogbait, stupid quadruped, Bond, James Bond.

TOPSY: Humans love names. I'm Topsy. How ridiculous is that? I could be a rabbit. But they think Topsy is the tops. [*Cat guttural growling*] I'm so annoyed I've clawed the back of their couch to shreds. Where are you prowling?

TIGA: I have to find my way to the flames in the sky.

TOPSY: What's wrong with you? Why would you do that? It's why I appreciate Hawthorn. It's quiet and comfy. But I've heard west by the nasty wet-wet, there's flames in the ground that shoot up to the sky.

TIGA: Can you smell the salt of the sea on the wind there?

TOPSY: What's the sea?

TIGA: Forever water lapalap under the sky.

> TOPSY *caterwauls in horror.*

I have to find my owner Wanker.

TOPSY: Dogs are so needy. Share the love around. After I've had breakfast as they call it, it's a bit of canned smell, I make my way to the bowl of home-cooked food up the road, a scratch on the door, a meow and there it is. I'm considering moving in. I have beds, pats and snacks all over the neighbourhood. My servants are over the moon when I waltz back home. I'm still deciding if I'll stay. They need to lift their game. Topsy!!!

TIGA: But Wanker laughs and laughs. He's a workaholic student climate scientist who's going to change the world.

TOPSY: How?

TIGA: There's dogbright in his heart.

TOPSY: Does he like cats?

TIGA: Oh yes. He loves Squeaky. I do too. She sounds like a mouse with cheese. And she purrs when she talks to me, even though she's human.

TOPSY: In that case I approve. Down the hill is a long flat road. It's that way. Someone will help. Now scram. I want to be alone.

> TOPSY THE CAT *hisses and retreats back into her hidey-hole.*

> *Soundscape. Lighting change as* TIGA *travels on, seeking his way back home.*

TIGA: Hurry down hill.
    Silent houses yawn.
    Cracked pavements beat against my paws.
    Shadow tree holding stars,
    Dog barking, shut up, window bang.
    Fox, bushy tail jaunty, trots,
    Chase him,
    Howls.
    Howl back miserable,
    Cold wind blows,
    Now wet slashes.
    Lips curl,
    Smell apple pie floating in puddle wet
    Sodden, swallow, gulp it down.
    Swish, swish, swish cars sweep past,
    Headlights shine in eyes,
    Come so fast.
    Run and weave just miss
    The metal speeding at me.
    Drench me dripping damp.
    Paper bag blows, chase.
    Nowhere to roll all rough hard
    Battered, broken
    Smell the place I want to sleep.
    Curl up outside door with rich meaty smells.
    In the dogdark
    Dream I'm home.
    I open my eyes

Foot nudges me
My heart skips a beat.
Standing in the doorway.
Wanker!

Sound / lights change. Early morning outside the butcher's shop in Elsternwick, in heavy rain.

Watching sheets of rain. Lost in thought.
I smell him. Smells of sawdust.
He's not my Wanker.

BONES THE BUTCHER: [*Scottish accent*]: What's the matter boy? Are you lost?

TIGA: So cold. Shivering…

MISS LENTILS approaches, holding her hands over her head as if shielding herself from the rain.

MISS LENTILS: Can I stand under your awning?

BONES THE BUTCHER: A butcher's awning welcomes one and all.

MISS LENTILS: Oh! I'm a bit shy. Though you wouldn't think it. Me standing so close and borrowing your awning. I just felt safe you see. A man and his dog.

TIGA whimpers.

All this lightning and thunder.

BONES THE BUTCHER: Even the dog's scared. If there was a flood I could save you both!

MISS LENTILS: Yes. No. But your dog will protect us.

BONES: He's not mine. Got no tag.

MISS LENTILS: Oh the poor thing.

TIGA: Smells of flowers. Roses. Sweet and warm. I like the way she rubs my ears.

BONES THE BUTCHER: Over the rooftops there, a rainbow.

MISS LENTILS: [*glancing shyly at him*] If we were trapped here for weeks by rising water I'd give up lentils and give meat a go.

BONES THE BUTCHER: [*momentarily at a loss for words as he stares at her*] Meat's good for you. Lots of iron. [*Embarrassed, he looks away and pats* TIGA.] Poor woofers here would like a big feed. How thin he is. Bony.

MISS LENTILS: Can I buy him a hamburger patty?
TIGA: That'd be good.
   What a lovely lady you are Miss Lentils.
   But how about a leg of lamb?
BONES THE BUTCHER: Nice steaks today.
   I could go home and have my wife cook them tonight. But I'm all alone.
MISS LENTILS: No you're not. You have a dog now.
   The following dialogue overlaps on forward slash.
BONES THE BUTCHER: [*together*] Wouldn't be fair/
   I'm at work all day.
TIGA: [*together*] Steaks. Rich juicy dripping… I'd be happy to lie on the mat and smell the…
MISS LENTILS: [*together*] I'll adopt him. Her? / Oh. Is that silly?
TIGA: [*together*] Her? Did she say her? / Roll over, expose my under parts.
BONES THE BUTCHER: [*together*] It's romantic.
TIGA: [*together*] I'm a *he* / with no balls, lady.
MISS LENTILS: [*together*] He might die / otherwise.
TIGA: [*together*] Pat my tummy. While I smell those yummy fatty white chops.
BONES: How would you get him home?
MISS LENTILS: I'm on the train. Sandringham.
TIGA: Beef sausage, chicken sausage, I'd even go a vegan sausage.
MISS LENTILS: I'll say he's in training as a guide dog. But it's an orderly train line no-one questions you.
BONES: Has anyone ever told you, you have the most beautiful wee smile? Sorry that's a bit over the top.
MISS LENTILS: No it's not. If a dog likes a man, he must be normal. Nice.
BONES: I've never been married.
MISS LENTILS: Me neither.
BONES: I've never proposed.
MISS LENTILS: That's what lovers do.
BONES: When they're in love.
MISS LENTILS: They cook steaks not lentils.

TIGA: I'm drooling already.
BONES: And meet after work.
MISS LENTILS: And walk on the beach.

The following dialogue overlaps.

BONES: [*together*] We could do that if we went to your place. / Walk your new dog on the beach.

TIGA: [*together*] Please forget manners. What's wrong with you? Smell her warm wet hair. See how she just buried her face in my fur.

MISS LENTILS: [*together*] I think I'll go home with my new dog right now and wait for you to finish work / and meet me in Sandringham.

TIGA: [*together*] Do the same. Get on with it! Do it!

BONES: We'd be like a husband and wife.

    Sitting down to tea.

MISS LENTILS: Getting to know each other.

TIGA: Move closer! More love in the eyes! Watch me! Smile! Now melt with love! That's it. Pat me too. Tickle tummy, more like catgut it's so empty. And now your hands closer together and yes!

    Look at that!

    Holding hands.

    Finally she's buying steaks… big steaks… bloody newspaper and woofle the intestines for me. Follow her obediently to Sandringham.

    And that's how I end up in the rattling train. Marrowbone, slurping.

    Guts feeling nice and comfy.

    They don't need me now… job done. They've found each other!

BONES THE BUTCHER *and* MISS LENTILS *exit together.*

Lighting change. Soundscape as TIGA *searches for home.*

I run off the train and down the path.

    Seagulls flocking no time to play.

    Have to find Wanker by end of day.

    I'm mad possessed.

    Get out my way

    You pack of sweaty cyclists.

    Go to mow them down barking wildly.

    Plastic bottle thrown, it bounces, catch it, crunch it.

Keep heading down the track.
I'm never ever coming back.
Cock my leg, piss with glee,
Tiga was here; remember me,
The best dog out of the West.
In the low light chasing joggers like rabbits.
Swerving to avoid me. Cussing, call the Council!
Unpredictable. This track is meant to be dog free.
Running like a champion, swift as tiger.
Bite the wind. Snap it's icy cold.
Crawl under the pier. I am so stuffed!
Sit and watch the penguins, tumbling out the waves and stumbling home.
Homesick. Dogdark freezing. Rummage rubbish bins, smell of fish and chips, tear the paper,
Wanker's chippies best of all.
Dark and bright and bright and dark
Hunt him! Find him! Cars and highway.
Go dumpster diving with a feral in a bin
'Steakhouse St Kilda, its amazing dude. Want to stay?
Best food in an industrial bin you'll ever get?'
It's my idea of heaven but Wanker waits.
Up the road, spaghetti tangle, screeching metal, dinging wheels,
Smell the golf green, hear the honking swans, no time to chase.
Head down the road bright as fire.
Big pictures hanging in the sky. Where's the flames?
Follow the tunnel under the road.
I know this tunnel! Crown Casino!
Gates of Mammon! Packer's hell.
Wanker always drives this way and swears,
'We are never ever going there.'
Yet this is wagging crazy here am I!
So I'm close!
What???
My maps all scrambled up in my head.
There's the flames
But where's the oil tanks? Where's the fire stacks reaching high.

> This is weak flames a whooshing.
> Benches, food and coloured lights, people, mouths-a-gaping, walking by.
> I'm going crazy as a west wind blow the smells of home.
> I'm nearly there!
> Crashing through the dogdark, swim under the bridge,
> Sun coming up. Suburban streets.
> Row after row
> Sniff around.
> I found it!

Soundscape out and lights change.

The weatherboard house, with gutters hanging down.
> The smelly storm water drain.
> The picket fence all torn.
> The spiky soft bush and…

A towel is thrown. TIGA *puts it around his shoulders.*

My ratty towel lying on the ground.
> Wanker always rubs my paws and under my belly and the top of my head.
> I'M HOME.

TIGA *is at a stranger's weatherboard house in Port Melbourne.*

CASEY *enters with a laundry basket and is horrified to see* TIGA.

CASEY: ALF! There's a giant Doberman! Alfonso!
ALFONSO: What?
CASEY: It's coming closer. It's going to bite me. It's getting ready to bite.
ALFONSO: Get inside. I'll call the dogcatcher.
CASEY: I can't, it's got me cornered. It's going to take a huge lump out of me I know it. Help me! Help me. GET AWAY.
TIGA: Who are you? Where's Wanker?
CASEY: Its mouth is open, ready to go me.
TIGA: What's happened to Wanker?
CASEY: So many teeth. He'll tear me to pieces in the backyard.
TIGA: Am I in the wrong place?
CASEY: Do something, can't you hear him barking at me. He's terrorising me.

TIGA: Can I have a pat?
CASEY: [*throwing shirt at* TIGA] Get out of my face.
TIGA: Stop waving the shirt in my face. Whipity flicking it at me.
CASEY: ALLFFFONSO… What are you doing you useless good for nothing.
TIGA: What do you want me to do? Get it out of my face.
CASEY: He's got the shirt. He's ripping it to shreds. It'll be me next.
ALFONSO: Calm down babes. Take a step back.
CASEY: Get out here.

  TIGA *woofles*.

ALFONSO: No way.
CASEY: [*throwing sheet*] He's going to maul me. Call the police. He's going crazy.
TIGA: I want to get out of here. Get out of my way.
CASEY: He's attacking the sheets.

  CASEY *and* TIGA *both grab the sheet tugging it back and forth.*

ALFONSO: Don't move. It can smell your fear.
CASEY: Stop staring at me.
TIGA: Stop eyeballing me.
CASEY: I hate you, you bastard. LEAVE ME ALONE.
TIGA: Leave me alone.
CASEY: I'm so scared.
TIGA: Stop throwing shit at me. I'm getting all confused.
CASEY: [*falling to her knees*] I hate dogs. Hate them.
TIGA: What have I done wrong? What's the matter? Get away!
ALFONSO: Throw the laundry basket at him.
CASEY: He'll bite me bad. Just like when I was a kid. Getting bites all over me. They're vicious killers. Stop him, Stop him.

  CASEY *hides her head under the laundry basket.*

TIGA: There's a poi-ing sound in the air.
ALFONSO: Poi-ing.

  TIGA *yelps*.

TIGA: And then a cut. A slash. A stab. Blood red is running down. Stab and stab.
ALFONSO: That got him.

Lighting state changes as GRUFF GIRL *enters. She lives in the house next door to* CASEY *and* ALFONSO.

GRUFF GIRL: What is going on? You're waking up the whole street! What are you doing? You dickhead what you shoot him for? He's a nice looking dog and you've just stuffed him up. You mongrel.

ALFONSO: What are you talking about?

TIGA: There's an arrow in my leg you shot me you shot me.

GRUFF GIRL: It's a crying shame. There's someone over the road that might like this dog. You could have killed it. It's a pedigree dog. Now look at him. He's gone all woozy. Passed out. I'll look after him.

TIGA injured blacks out.

Dream lighting state. POODLE *and* KELPIE *appear. They growl at* TIGA.

TIGA: I can hear Kelpie and Poodle. They are here. They stand on the edge of the darkness and growl. I don't like Kelpie and Poodle. They're trouble. Go 'em before they go me. But it's like I'm in slow motion walking in treacle.

POODLE: I want to promenade with dainty feet down Port Melbourne docks.

KELPIE: Yeah knock off time! What's to knock off? Knock off?

POODLE: Luxury goods like him.

KELPIE: How'd he get here? Get here?

POODLE: He's a new pedigree breed. A Dobie. An outsider.

TIGA: But in my lineage—

KELPIE: What's a lineage? Speak Aussie, sunshine. He must be a foreigner.

POODLE: German. Full of germs. Rotten stinky hunden. But he think's he's William Tell with that arrow in him. Or Robin Hood.

TIGA: I'm a Westie born under the Altona tanks.

Howls of disapproval from POODLE *and* KELPIE.

POODLE: I spend all my time lounging on the lounge eating biccies and reading encyclopaedias. You were bred so no-one would attack the taxman.

KELPIE: What's a taxman?

POODLE: A man who takes lots of money from most men to give to a few men. He's elitist. Bourgeois.
KELPIE: Is that good? Is that good?
POODLE: Prick Ears you are the great unwashed—
KELPIE: That's good. That's good.
POODLE: Your sort would hate him. Attack!
KELPIE: Weak as piss. Is it a ewe or a ram pretending to be a dog?
TIGA: Hang on! NAAH! Stop! I'm working class! Like you Kelpie! I've a bit of greyhound in me.
KELPIE: That's all right then. We'll take a bet on yer. How fast can yer run sunshine?
TIGA: Show me the rabbit!
KELPIE: If you don't win its off to the knacker's yard and the Pal can for you. Those big machines will grind you up into a brown lumpy squishy jelly. Like all the sheep.

    I'll give you a head start. Before I come after you. Head west... follow the sun sunny boy.

> KELPIE *exits,* POODLE *exits the other way.*

POODLE: You're on the wrong side of the street. You are such a loser.

> *Lighting state changes as* TIGA *comes to. He finds himself in a dark alley with* GRUFF GIRL. *She meets* SLOUCHY *in the shadows.*

TIGA: Different place. Different smells. What happened to looking after me?
GRUFF GIRL: You put the word out on the street and I've found what you want. This one'll protect you.
SLOUCHY: I don't want vet bills.
GRUFF GIRL: He'll be fine. Five hundred.
SLOUCHY: You're kidding.

> TIGA'*s dialogue overlaps with the following.*

GRUFF GIRL: These dogs go for a grand.
TIGA: Wanker bought me because he loved me. I don't get a good feeling about this.
SLOUCHY: Three hundred.
GRUFF GIRL: Four hundred.
TIGA: Smells wrong. Chickenfed man.

SLOUCHY: How fierce is he?
GRUFF GIRL: Really fierce. He's a Doberman.
TIGA: Mum said we are big prick dogs.
SLOUCHY: Doberman? He's got a tail. Why's he got a tail?
GRUFF GIRL: It's a law now.
TIGA: Even if I was the littlest.
SLOUCHY: It's a big tail.
TIGA: Sometimes…
GRUFF GIRL: Yeah but he can't do nothing with it.
SLOUCHY: He could knock the cup off my table.
GRUFF GIRL: Keep him outside.
SLOUCHY: What if I want him inside?
GRUFF GIRL: Get a bigger table.
SLOUCHY: He doesn't look like an SS dog.
TIGA: You have to bare your teeth…
GRUFF GIRL: He's German.
SLOUCHY: They look alert the Nazi killer dogs, pointy ears.
TIGA: More! Look like you mean it…
GRUFF GIRL: He'll hear every sound.
TIGA: Big teeth!
SLOUCHY: Can you clip his ears now?
GRUFFGIRL: He'll just bleed everywhere. It won't work.
TIGA: Don't be such a scaredy cat!
SLOUCHY: Yeah but he don't look scary. It's his job to be scary and he looks like a sook with his big tail and floppy ears.
TIGA: Westie number nine…
GRUFF GIRL: I'll show you scary. Step on his tail.
TIGA: BIG TEETH!

> TIGA *yelps then snarls.*

GRUFF GIRL: That's seriously scary.
SLOUCHY: Three hundred and thirty and not a cent more.
GRUFF GIRL: Deal.

> GRUFF GIRL *exits. Lighting change.* TIGA *is now trapped with* SLOUCHY *who is at home watching television.*

SLOUCHY: MMM. That Samantha's a bit of alright.

TIGA: Day in day out Chickenfed's home and buried in that bright screen. Stalk him. On my belly. Creep up on him. Surprise him!
SLOUCHY: Piss off!
TIGA: Can I have some of that big bucket of chicken? If I beg? Look I can beg.
SLOUCHY: That's funny.

Throws nuggets at TIGA.

Catch the nugget. What's wrong with your neck, floppy? I've got a dud dog.
TIGA: It's just stiff. Won't stretch and flick. Come on! Throw to me.
SLOUCHY: Lazy good for nothing. Entertain me!
TIGA: I can catch. It's just a bit painful. Come on! Nuggets! Nuggets!
SLOUCHY: Don't you eye off my Kentucky Fried. You're getting none of this floppy if you can't catch! [*Chasing* TIGA *out*] Go on! Out the backyard with you. Or I'll step on that tail.

Lighting change. Out in the backyard at SLOUCHY*'s place.*

TIGA: I know what you are... fence of the back yard. You're trapping me. Making me a prisoner. Mum wouldn't want me to be a prisoner. So Chickenfed can step on my tail again. Hurting me. Hiding me from Wanker... Shut Chickenfed's bite trap for good. This isn't what I'm meant to be. Some sad-dogs prisoner. I'm gonna climb you, scale you... cling onto you... again... again...nearly there... haul meself up you. Whoah! Look down there's a mighty drop... and... fallllllinng down... leg gives way... but...

Go, go, go... I'm out of the prison...

Lights change/ sound comes up as TIGA *struggles on into the darkness, running.*

See Mum!
 Westie number nine is free!
 Run before he gets me.
 Racing to the sea.
 Stretch every sinew.
 Breath bursting.
 My head bobbing... water stings... Smell of dark oily... clogs my nose and fur... all matted

Take the water by the throat.
Charge onto the flames in the sky.
Lights shining in the tall shapes behind.
Straining every muscle in my neck
Keep afloat.
Scrabble onto sand and mud and spiky grass.
World is sleeping.
Rats are squeaking.
Home is calling.
Footsore. Limping.

Lights fade. Soundscape out.

No moon.
Limping badly.
He's walking home in the dogdark.
Bag on his back.
Follow him. He stops.
Shines his torch in my eyes.

TIGA *on the streets of Spotswood at night encounters* BUS DRIVER *walking home after his shift.*

BUS DRIVER: I knew you were following me. I got eyes in the back of my head.
What's the matter with you?
Who hurt you?
I won't hurt you.
Lot of hurting out here.
Want a bed for the night?
Come with me Friend.
You've got a nasty wound. Like me.
With that limp you need to stay inside.
You'll feel better Friend.

Lighting change. TIGA *is inside the* BUS DRIVER*'s house.*

Safer inside.
I need you to help.
See this equipment.
Cameras.

You'll hear them outside.
I'm being followed.
They get on the bus. The brothers.
Psych me out. Press the ticket against the reader and stare at me. You know we are coming to get you.
Sit behind me. Breathing hard. I hear their thoughts.
They're coming any day now.

BUS DRIVER *whispers to himself.*

They want the house.

Scribbles on the walls.

I've saved all my life for this house and now they want it.

TIGA: Bus driver draws marks on the wall. Hundreds of them.

BUS DRIVER: [*agitated*] Have to watch the cameras. Who came to the house today Friend?

TIGA: No-one. The house feels hot. It makes me sleepy

BUS DRIVER: Don't go near the front door on my day off. Dangerous.

TIGA: I sleep next to him.
Without him. He leaves for hours
Next to him…
Without him.
Next to him
Nothing else to do.
It's hotter and hotter.

BUS DRIVER: They want to take everything off me.

TIGA: Nuzzle him. Open the windows.

BUS DRIVER: Close the curtains. They're out there with their long lens cameras. Watching my every move. We have to hide in the attic. Won't find us there. Make it look like no-one's home.

Lighting change.

TIGA: I can't get up these tiny stairs. Slippery rungs. Claws slide. He tries to pull me up. Not strong enough. He's up there alone. I whine come down.

BUS DRIVER: Brothers want to kill me. But I'm a step ahead of them. See this rope. Tie it here nice and tight. Have to be careful.

TIGA: [*whining*] Come down.

BUS DRIVER: I know why I brought you here. You're my friend. My only witness.
>Stop staring at me.
>You're making it harder.
>Breaking my heart with those beautiful eyes.
>
>BUS DRIVER *crosses back to* TIGA *and hugs him.*

I can't leave you here alone can I?
>You depend on me, don't you friend?
>
>*Pause.*

TIGA: Put your head against my belly. Like I used to with my Mum.
BUS DRIVER: [*lying next to* TIGA] I won't leave you tonight. How can there be so much warmth in a cold nose?
>Stop staring at me… they hurt me those beautiful eyes.
>What will I do friend?
>Is there help?
>
>BUS DRIVER *exits.*

TIGA: Goes out quietly locks the door.

>TIGA *lies stretched out on his belly and watches where* BUS DRIVER *has exited.*

Are humans like dogs? Has he gone looking for his mum?
>Don't move.
>Wait for him
>Keep watch.
>Wait.
>Wait.
>WAIT.
>Count rabbits…
>Hanging off the ceiling, bouncing on the lino.
>Peeping behind the curtains.
>Burrowing in the cushions.
>Close my eyes.
>When we were pups…
>Mum told us.
>
>*Lighting change for* TIGA*'s memory of his MUM.*

TIGA'S MUM: There was this Lab I met.
> Had a diamond collar and lived in a big mansion in Toorak.
> Owners put in all these palm trees in the garden for the dog to pee against.
> The Labrador mooched around all day.
> I met her in a car park at a Collingwood game.
> Owners mad Magpie supporters.
> The rich don't see what we see.
> They come to this football ground.
> The rich think it's all equal here.

TIGA: But they don't see the misery.

TIGA'S MUM: They know nothing about what goes on in the real world as they eat out of their fancy dog bowls. It's a life of barbeques with chops. Make mine medium rare. Hold the salad. No dried food for them.
> WESTIES have to battle every day if we want to eat at all.

Lighting black out as TIGA'S MUM *disappears.*

The BUS DRIVER*'s house is now getting darker.*

TIGA: I eat some old stale cornflakes soggy with milk. Belching badly.
> And a half eaten pizza gives me the burps.
> Bark at the rattling windows. The hum of the fridge. Every car that passes.
> Scratch at the door. Do poos on the newspaper. Guts churning.
> The Bus Company rings and rings. Leave long messages.
> No-one else rings.
> The flies are buzzing. Snap. Buzzing around my ears. Eating them alive.
> Snap. Snap.
> There's banging on the door.
> They break in.
> I don't make a sound.

> *TIGA cowers in the corner.*

POLICE ONE: Nice looking dog.

POLICE TWO: Useless guard dog. What's the matter with him? Why's he hiding under the table?

POLICE ONE: Traumatised.
POLICE TWO: No good to anyone.
POLICE ONE: C'mon mate.
POLICE TWO: What's all the snarly shit?
POLICE ONE: Just ignore the dog. Put some food down.
TIGA: I cower against the back wall. Dig my claws in.

> *The* POLICE *trap* TIGA, *pull him out and throw him into the middle of the space. Lighting change as* TIGA *finds himself at a rescue home for dogs.*

Another wire prison.
   Yelping
   Barking
   Howling
   Wailing
   Whining.
   Humans passing.
   No-one looking.
   The horror in the yard
   Unspoken.
   No-one's coming.
   Some crouch
   Some wait
   Some wag their tails
   Eyes shining
   FIND me!
   Poke my nose through the wire netting.

> BLUE HEELER *crawls slowly out from a narrow entrance.*

Old Bluey's staring at his bowl
   Biscuits untouched.
BLUE HEELER: If you don't get picked it'll be the end of you.
TIGA: What is the end?
BLUE HEELER: They give you the green dream.
TIGA: What is that?
BLUE HEELER: The end.
TIGA: Of what?
BLUE HEELER: Of your misery because no human wants you.

TIGA: And what happens then?
BLUE HEELER: There's a big open pit and they shovel all the dog carcasses in.

And no-one visits you no more. All the bones of the forgotten dogs endlessly piled on top of each other. Old soldiers, who have done their duty by making owners happy.

TIGA: Is it ever different?
BLUE HEELER: I don't know. Most of us are born, suffer and die.
TIGA: What's that chalky circle on your head?
BLUE HEELER: They are going to get upset when they have to do what they are going to do to you, poor things.
TIGA: What does the E in the middle mean?
BLUE HEELER: Exit with dignity. You have to show them how.

BLUE HEELER crawls back into the narrow entrance.

TIGA: No-one came for Bluey.

Lighting becomes brighter. SPONGE WOMAN *enters with big sponge. She is cheerful and breezy.*

SPONGE WOMAN: You need a bath!

SPONGE WOMAN *is a dog rescue home worker.*

TIGA: Naah! Bath! Don't want a bath.
SPONGE WOMAN: Don't want you smelling. You have to look nice.

She enthusiastically sponges him all over.

Stay still! You're a lucky fella! There's a chip!
TIGA: I hear The EJ.
I hear that rattle rattle engine.
I hear his footsteps.
That wonderful Wanker comes for me!
Rolls his ciggie between his fingers.
My heart stops.
It's the best moment in my life!
WANKER: Yeah that's him. Tiga Waggers.
TIGA: I'm going crazy with joy. Turning round and round in circles. Barking. Even give my tail a work out. Round and round. He came back!
WANKER: Where did you find him? It's been ages. Poor fellow. What's happened to him? Oh Waggers you poor thing!

SPONGE WOMAN: His tail is fractured. Someone's put the boot in probably steel cap. His hind leg looks like he's had some implement stuck in it. He's lucky that whatever it was didn't paralyse him. And he looks like he's been half starved.

> WANKER *kneels by* TIGA *stroking and patting him.*

TIGA: Is my old pongy black sheepskin rug still under the kitchen cupboards?

WANKER: Yes.

TIGA: Are the old half chewed bones still in the backyard? My fake grass turf bed under the giant gum tree?

WANKER: Yes mate.

TIGA: My tennis balls?

My rat shit chewed up basketball?

WANKER: Yes, yes.

SQUEAKY: Jump in the car!

> *Lighting change as* TIGA *and* WANKER *are now in the car with* SQUEAKY.

Tiga! Beautiful boy.

TIGA: I jump at her, lick her. Shadow both of them. Bursting with joy. [TIGA *is behind* SQUEAKY *hanging onto her shoulder. His tongue is hanging out.*] We go to the beach. I can smell the sea. I whimper and witter in the back seat. Stand up. Rock side to side. Stick my head out the window.

And slobber. Saliva pours over Squeaky's head.

SQUEAKY: Sit Tiga! Sit down.

TIGA: I can't! I can smell rotting seaweed. Heaven! Out the car.

> *Soundscape. Bright lighting. It's a beautiful, perfect day at the beach.*

I stretch my good legs out.

WANKER: Not so fast. Come back!

TIGA: I'm running! Look at me run!

Down at the sandy edge. Wanker throws the ball across the channel and into the mud.

Watch me go!

Leap into that salty water and swim against the current.

The jellyfish and the ibis above my head sweeping the sky with their wings.

Into that mud flats and lift my paws. Plop plop.

And back in, head up. Fight the water.

WANKER: He's so funny.

TIGA: Throw the ball! Throw the ball again! Standing on my back legs in the water.

SQUEAKY: Go Tiga!

TIGA: Bobbing on the waves. The ball.

Salt in my nose and mouth.

Head up.

Up the bank shake the water out.

Next to them.

SQUEAKY: Not near me! You're soaking me.

WANKER: There's a whole beach Tiga!

TIGA: Look at me go the seagulls

I'm going to catch a seagull… what's to eat?

SQUEAKY: What's he found?

TIGA: An old, mouldy, stinky biscuit, yuk that didn't taste real good.

WANKER: One more ball. Run you dry. Or you'll stink the car out. It's time to go home.

TIGA: Home? Get the chippies! Chippies for supper.

SQUEAKY: Chippies!

WANKER and SQUEAKY eating chips.

TIGA: Love hot chips wrapped in newspaper.

Put the chips in my mouth. Now. I'm hungry.

WANKER: Gentle! Don't be greedy. You almost took my fingers.

Back home in WANKER and SQUEAKY's house in Altona. Night.

SQUEAKY: It's time for our bath.

TIGA: That's when their skin goes all soft and wrinkly and smells like fruit.

SQUEAKY: Wash away all the stress of losing you.

TIGA: Yes! Wanker's bath time. My favourite!

In the bath, SQUEAKY and WANKER sit opposite each other.

WANKER: You are torturing me! This water is so hot!

SQUEAKY: It feels cold.
WANKER: It's burning. No more!
TIGA: Lick!
SQUEAKY: Lie back.
TIGA: Lick!
WANKER: What the…! Go away Tiga!
TIGA: Lick!
SQUEAKY: Don't flick water at him.
TIGA: Lick!
WANKER: He's standing there licking my back! You're encouraging him. Go away!
TIGA: Lick! Hide behind the door. I come back and give another big lick.
WANKER: Get away crazy dog.
SQUEAKY: He just wants to be a part of it.
WANKER: I love him to death but he's a lunatic dog and I don't need him to be part of this bath.
SQUEAKY: He's getting you clean.
WANKER: The dog is as insane as my partner.
TIGA: Lick!
WANKER: Tiga! Stop it!
TIGA: Little lick.

Lighting changes to the darkness of late night, everyone has gone to bed.

Funny in the dogdark… Not right. Head hurts… throb throb throb.
Look for Wanker in the dogdark…
I love him.
Let me [*howling*] out.
Gets his big torch.
Puts on his dressing gown and stumbles out to the kitchen.
He opens the back door.
I stumble.

WANKER *and* TIGA *outside in the garden at night.*

WANKER: Forgetting why we're here?
TIGA: Looks at me and I look at him.
Under the moonlight.

WANKER: Hurry up. It's cold.
TIGA: It is.
WANKER: Don't muck around Tiga.
TIGA: I'm not.

> WANKER *goes back to bed.*

Back inside.
> Back to bed.
> What am I doing?
> Smell the lino. Mice in the walls.
> Lie down.
> I can't.
> How do legs do that?

> *Woofles and howls.* WANKER *comes back.*

WANKER: What is it? I have an exam in the morning. And I can't even work out what's wrong with you.

> WANKER *and* TIGA *go outside again and stare at each other.*

Stop messing me around.
TIGA: Why do we keep coming out here?
> He waits.
> I wait.
> We wait.
WANKER: When I'm inside I can't sleep. Now I'm out here I'm so tired. I'll fail my exam tomorrow, I don't know enough. Only that the world's fucked...

> WANKER *sitting down looks up at the night sky.* TIGA *is curled up with his head in* WANKER*'s lap.*

Up there the stars, we're made of stars and dark matter... that light it's not a star, because it's moving. It's the international space station.
TIGA: Everything is spinning. Bones compressing. What's happening?
WANKER: There because of sputnik... how to wage war from space.
TIGA: Mum said push through whatever life throws your way, catch it, chase it.
WANKER: Russians put a dog into a space capsule, shot her into the stratosphere. Was it possible for life to survive up there, to fight a war?

TIGA: Paws won't push out, all collapsed. Darkness beneath me.
WANKER: The first one killed was her. Pounded by gravity or burnt to a cinder when crashing back to earth. No-one was told that of course. The wonder was a dog in space. Our hearts are stone Tiga. But she went because she was so gentle. A little stray dog from the streets of Moscow, who wanted to be loved and did whatever was needed. The only one who helped the scientists by getting into smaller and smaller test capsules. Obedient to the end.
TIGA: Pain making me wilt and curl like a leaf. [*Woofling.*] I woofle. He wants me to understand.
WANKER: On the last afternoon—
TIGA: Sun warm on my fur not cold like now.
WANKER: The scientist took her home to play with his children.
TIGA: Like sinking in dark water, struggle to breathe.
WANKER: So she'd have a beautiful memory.
TIGA: His hand scratching my ears.
WANKER: In the terror.
TIGA: If only I could walk, I'd be alright. Did I do something wrong?
WANKER: After the dog Laika, it was men, we followed. We need you to show us the way wherever we wander.
TIGA: Over the dirt Mum said. Dirt keeps you strong. Just smell the earth. It's all there is.
WANKER: The Dog Star sees her, quantum particles in our blue orb. I know. I know I don't know anything. I'm just a wannabe climate scientist who peddles in make believe. It must be morning, see the mudlark's nest. It's a perfect circle. Inside.
TIGA: Shuddering and shaking
>Back legs keep collapsing.
>Drunk.
>Fall again.

>*Lighting changes as morning comes.* SQUEAKY *enters.* TIGA *falls and can't get up*

SQUEAKY: Tiga! UP!
TIGA: Big effort… jump.
>Then fall.
>Stand.

Fall again.
Squeaky's panicking.
Wanker picks me up.

TIGA *is put in the car.*

Puts me in the EJ.
Where we going?

WANKER: I remember him sitting in his little glass box. Waiting for someone to come along and buy him. To love him. Looking at me so hopefully with those big brown eyes. I can't leave him now.

SQUEAKY: You have to do your exam. You've worked so hard all these years. I'm with him. He'll be alright. He's going to get healthy.

WANKER exits. Lighting change as SQUEAKY gets TIGA to Lort Smith Animal Hospital.

TIGA: Antiseptic smells. I've been here before.
Are you going to put my balls back? If there's ball donors, can I have the really big huge ones…?

SQUEAKY: C'mon, c'mon. The vet'll make you better. Like before!

TIGA: Don't mention before.

SQUEAKY: You will won't you? Make him better?

In the consulting room TIGA lying on his side, VET and SQUEAKY on either side of him.

VET: Can he stand at all?

SQEAKY: A bit.

VET: Strange he seems drunk. Do you grow dope?

SQUEAKY: No!

VET: Weed poisons dogs, can make them sick. Maybe he ate some.

SQUEAKY: Maybe.

VET: Maybe someone threw a hash cookie into the yard.

SQUEAKY: Maybe.

VET: Did he ingest chemicals, or paints maybe?

SQUEAKY: Maybe someone threw poison bait over the fence?

VET: Maybe. We'll keep him in overnight… [*To self*] It could be a lumbar number 5.

[*Comforting* SQUEAKY] Sudden onset… rare. Poor fellow. He's a beautiful dog. Lets hope for the best. If he's eaten something it'll work through his system and he'll be right as rain, just like that, maybe.

Exit SQUEAKY *and* VET.

TIGA: Why have they left me here?

They shave my leg. Put the drip in. Nose check, ears check...

Ten, nine, eight, seven, sticks...

But in the night I can see into the shadows. Kelpie's sitting there panting.

I don't like Prick Ears and Poodle.

Sound and lighting change. TIGA *medicated and sleepy senses* KELPIE *and* POODLE *are with him.*

KELPIE: Time to go. Nip you. Nudge you out of life.

POODLE: Humans don't like death. They like colour, conversation and life.

If you die now it'd be the polite thing to do. Save them the shock.

KELPIE: From seeing you on your side like a flyblown sheep.

POODLE: It's a casebook example of wobblers, common to Dobermans, gets 'em young, poor genetic stock.

KELPIE: Round him up, git up, git up, why's his neck all floppy?

POODLE: Collapsed. Like his legs.

KELPIE: I'll sink my teeth into that neck if you don't git. Git!

TIGA *snarls.*

TIGA: How do I know it's true?

POODLE: Because I say so.

KELPIE: You listen to him. Or you'll regretit. Regretit. Go on die.

TIGA: I don't want to—

KELPIE: I don't want to. Lardydah. We don't want youse around. You're not wanted. Wanted.

POODLE: You should never have been born. A disgrace to any right thinking Doberman. Weak as a piss-about on pistewatered down wine. Your mother must be ashamed she gave birth to you.

TIGA: I'm not going!

POODLE: Why fight me and Prick Ears? Let the owners remember you how you were. Fit, healthy, sparkling eyes.

KELPIE: Not all frozen like a sheep carcass hanging in the abattoir.

TIGA: I want to see them one last time.
KELPIE: They don't want to see you. Too horrible. They've gone for good.
POODLE: It was a mistake. We should never have taken him in the first place.
KELPIE: Return him. Return him. Get a better one.
TIGA: How do you know?
POODLE: There's no life left in you. Why would they bother?
KELPIE: What's left to say sunshine? That hasn't been said.
TIGA: I'll say goodbye.

> KELPIE *and* POODLE *vanish in the darkness leaving* TIGA *alone. Lights change.*

I can hear the EJ
> Their footsteps.
> Here they come.
> Lift my head.
> Takes all my strength.
> I love them.
> Big tears. Wanker's face so close to mine. Such big tears. Sploshing on his nose.

> *Soundscape.*

> WANKER *and* SQUEAKY *stand at a distance from* TIGA.

WANKER: I love you. From the moment you sat in my hand at the pet shop and peed all over it, your soft nose... your funny inward turning paws that bounced and bounced. Bounding... your flat out sprint chasing the tennis ball down... seeing you run wild... crazy with scents and sounds... paradise... you showed me... now your head in my hands looking at me with those big brown eyes... Don't go... beautiful boy... holding onto you so tight...

Every morning... your paw on my pillow... it's a new day lets explore... did I ever love you enough? Because you gave me so much love... and if I wake up tomorrow and you're not there it'll be like my heart's all torn apart.

SQUEAKY: How I love you, when you sit on my lap even though you're so big, and you let me scratch your tummy as you lie on your back with your big velvety ears, the whirlwind of you when we come home, all the joy, your tail, you spinning around us like crazy...

TIGA: The dogdark fills my eyes
Beat the green dream before it flows on in…
I'm not ready for the end.
Don't hold me down.
What would Mum say?
LEAP FOR YOUR LIFE.
Struggle up.
Legs move.
What will Squeaky and Wanker do without me?
They need me.
For them.
Up, up, up!
Mum didn't have us all pups,
So we'd go with out a fight.
Don't give Poodle and Kelpie the satisfaction
They were right.
Dodge the death smell
Cold and clammy.
Beautiful life, wait!
Jump into it! Hang onto it!
I love it here.
A rush of air.
I'm standing upright!
Turning and turning,
Swirling careful first, slow,
As if finding my feet
Faster now.
Swirling
Around and around.
With every turn of the dance
Becoming freer and freer…
Collar of pain breaks.
The dogbright fills me with joy.
Let's go chase sea gulls.

THE END

THE PARRICIDE

BY DIANE STUBBINGS

R.E. Ross Trust Award Winner
Shortlisted, Rodney Seaborn Playwrights' Award

CURRENCY Press • Sydney

CURRENT THEATRE SERIES

First published in 2014
by Currency Press Pty Ltd,
PO Box 2287, Strawberry Hills, NSW, 2012, Australia
enquiries@currency.com.au
www.currency.com.au

in association with La Mama Theatre

The Parricide copyright © Diane Stubbings, 2014

COPYING FOR EDUCATIONAL PURPOSES

The Australian *Copyright Act 1968* (Act) allows a maximum of one chapter or 10% of this book, whichever is the greater, to be copied by any educational institution for its educational purposes provided that that educational institution (or the body that administers it) has given a remuneration notice to Copyright Agency Limited (CAL) under the Act.

For details of the CAL licence for educational institutions contact CAL, Level 15, 233 Castlereagh Street, Sydney, NSW, 2000. Tel: within Australia 1800 066 844 toll free; outside Australia +61 2 9394 7600; Fax: +61 2 9394 7601; Email: info@copyright.com.au

COPYING FOR OTHER PURPOSES

Except as permitted under the Act, for example a fair dealing for the purposes of study, research, criticism or review, no part of this book may be reproduced, stored in a retrieval system, or transmitted in any form or by any means without prior written permission. All enquiries should be made to the publisher at the address above.

Any performance or public reading of *The Parricide* is forbidden unless a licence has been received from the author or the author's agent. The purchase of this book in no way gives the purchaser the right to perform the play in public, whether by means of a staged production or a reading. All applications for public performance should be addressed to the author c/– Currency Press.

NATIONAL LIBRARY OF AUSTRALIA CIP DATA

Title: Stray and The parricide / R Johns and Diane Stubbings.
ISBN: 9781925005097 (paperback)
Series: Current theatre series.
Other Authors/Contributors:
    Johns, R. Stray.
    Stubbings, Diane. The Parricide.

Printed by Fineline Print & Copy Service, St Peters, NSW.
Cover image: Vasily Perov, *Portrait of F.M Dostoyevsky*. Source: Google Art Project
Cover design by Peter Mumford.

Contents

THE PARRICIDE

Diane Stubbings 1

Theatre Program at the end of the playtext

The Parricide was first produced at La Mama Theatre, Melbourne, on 7 May 2014 with the following cast:

FEDYA	Lyall Brooks
ANNA/KATYA	Anneli Bjorasen
KOLYA/MITYA	Nick Simpson-Deeks
ELENA/GRUSHENKA	Odette Joannidis
KARAKOZOV/ALYOSHA	Gabriel Partington

Writer, Diane Stubbings
Director, Karen Berger
Dramaturg, Dave Letch

DEVELOPMENT

The Parricide had its first reading at Parnassus' Den (Sydney, May 2009) with the following cast and creatives:

FEDYA	Tony Sloman
ANNA	Sally Cahill
KOLYA	Anthony Phelan
ELENA	Linden Wilkinson
KARAKOZOV	Matt Minto
DIRECTOR	Dave Letch

The play had a second reading at Parnassus' Den (October 2010) with the following cast changes:

ANNA	Kate Worsley
KOLYA	Jonathan Hardy
KARAKOZOV	Gus Murray

As a result of funding provided by the R.E. Ross Trust, *The Parricide* was workshopped in October 2011, with a subsequent reading at fortyfivedownstairs (Melbourne, November 2013) involving the following cast and creatives:

FEDYA	David Pidd
ANNA/KATYA	Isabella Dunwill
KOLYA/MITYA	Nick Simpson-Deeks
ELENA/GRUSHENKA	Odette Joannidis
KARAKOZOV/ALYOSHA	Gabriel Partington
DIRECTOR	Karen Berger
DRAMATURG	Dave Letch
SOUND	David Joseph
LIGHTING	Andy Turner

WRITER'S NOTE

The Parricide is a work of fiction. Based on the life of one of the world's greatest novelists, it draws out from that life ideas about passion, fear and the creative instinct.

The writing of *The Parricide* began with Fyodor Dostoyevsky's formidable novel *The Brothers Karamazov*. Reading this story of three brothers whose father is murdered, I was captured both by the intricate dynamics of the Karamazov family and the intense courtroom drama that plays out in the novel's second half. But what most fascinated me—and what lingered long after I'd finished reading the novel—was the character of Ivan, the second of the Karamazov brothers.

While Dostoyevsky explicitly proffers Alexei, the youngest brother, as the hero of his novel, it was, for me, Ivan who gave the novel its emotional core. In Ivan's deep (yet unrequited) love for his brother's fiancée, there is something reminiscent of the great romantic heroes. But, more than that, I'd argue that it's Ivan's journey from conviction to doubt—and the ferocity of his intellectual engagement—that marks him as the true hero of *The Brothers Karamazov*.

Thinking about my own response to Dostoyevsky's novel, I began to wonder about the extent to which an author is really in control of their own work. Could it be that there are other forces that push the writing beyond the author's conscious control? Dostoyevsky might have told himself he was writing a novel about a young man—Alexei Karamazov—who finds truth and light in the form of the Christian God (and who in a projected, but never written, second volume goes on to kill the Tsar), but was Dostoyevsky, in fact, writing about something else entirely? Was it actually Ivan Karamazov—whose nihilism pulses so forcefully through the novel—who more fully captured Dostoyevsky's imagination? And was Dostoyevsky as wound up in this dangerous nihilism as Ivan himself was?

This is the ground out of which *The Parricide* grew; and, reading more about Dostoyevsky's life, I stumbled across a note which suggested that Dostoyevsky may have begun a draft of *The Brothers Karamazov* long before the final version was published. No trace of this earlier draft has ever been found (perhaps it did exist, perhaps it didn't), but the possibility that these ideas—about God, nihilism, jealousy, truth and faith—had been tumbling about in Dostoyevsky's mind for a very long time opened up all sorts of possibilities for me as a writer.

Researching Dostoyevsky's life further, I came across the charming story of how he met his second wife, Anna; and the sense of order and purpose she brought to his personal life offered a striking contrast to (what I saw as) the inherent disorder of Dostoyevsky's writing life. Bringing Dostoyevsky's wooing of Anna together with an early attempt to write *The Brothers Karamazov* seemed a promising way forward dramatically. But the play still wanted more.

I found what I needed in Dostoyevsky's arrest for conspiracy. Still in his twenties, and having just begun to make his mark in Russian letters, Dostoyevsky's subsequent imprisonment shaped both him and his writing more than anything else he'd experienced. What, I wondered, must it be like to emerge from ten years of virtual isolation in Siberia and have to re-establish your place in society; to re-assert yourself as a writer of note? And what happens to the revolutionary flame, the revolutionary spirit, after a man has been so long incarcerated in such extreme conditions? Is it doused completely, or is there a spark that persists? And, when political unrest again stalks the streets, is it a spark that, in a man like Dostoyevsky, is bound to be resurrected?

These are the questions which underpin *The Parricide*. In the writing of it—and over numerous drafts—I've moved a fair way from the known facts of Dostoyevsky's life, and I've telescoped several decades of history into a matter of weeks. This presented its own challenges: How to dramatise so many years of Russian history—and such a vast array of real and imagined characters—using only five actors?

Sometimes what at first seems like an intractable problem introduces all sorts of interesting possibilities. Seminal historical moments—such as the burning of St Petersburg—could be generated using light and sound effects. The tension between history and fabrication could be underscored by eschewing realistic sets and costumes in favour of something that gave both a modern and a historical sense. And rather than trying to hide the doubling of cast members, the actors' transitions from one character to another could be made explicit, the audience fully aware of the shifts in voice, gesture and costume, thereby magnifying the lines between the real and the imagined. Further, by having characters directly recounting to the audience their own versions of Dostoyevsky's life, it was possible to emphasise that the play is meant to be understood as a fiction—yet another rendering of Dostoyevsky's life story—rather than something historically factual.

Through all this, I've endeavoured to remain true to the spirit of the man and his writing, and if I've misjudged in any way, I take heart in the fact that Dostoyevsky's work will endure a lot longer than my own. At the very least, I hope *The Parricide* will entice people who don't know Dostoyevsky's work to discover his writing for themselves. The rewards of doing so are well worth the effort.

DIRECTOR'S NOTE

In October 2011, we were working on a script development of *The Parricide*. One morning, one of the actresses rang me, very flustered. There was a traffic jam on the freeway, she was running very late, but had I heard the news? There was a serious riot happening in Melbourne CBD! Her excitement was contagious and those of us already at rehearsal tuned in to listen to the battle between the police and Occupy Melbourne protestors. The energy and passion of that violence fed directly into our exploration of revolution in Dostoyevsky's Russia, making it more real, less 'historical'. We clearly saw that intense—sometimes violent—responses to an unjust society continue to happen. And though the Occupy movement is no longer active in Australia, the daily news from around the world forces us to think about the rights and wrongs of revolutionary activity.

The other aspect of *The Parricide* story that makes it so relevant to today (and every day) is the human relationships underlying societal forces. Playwright, Diane Stubbings, cleverly interweaves the stories of Dostoyevsky's *The Brothers Karamazov* and *The Gambler* with Dostoyevsky's relationships at the time of him meeting and marrying his second wife, Anna. Through this, she investigates the personal reasons for getting (or not getting) involved in social activism.

Dostoyevsky was a passionate and fascinating man: the initial moments of his ongoing epilepsy gave him instances of almost unbearable bliss; his addiction to gambling, where catastrophic losses meant he felt pure and inspired to write; his liaisons with some of Russia's most intellectual women. These subjects alone would make this play intriguing, but we also have the pleasure of investigating the genesis of some of his works of literary genius. Rich and dramatic territory indeed!

Karen Berger

ACKNOWLEDGEMENTS AND SOURCES

Particular thanks is owed to the R.E. Ross Trust and Parnassus' Den who have generously supported the development of this play.

Thanks also to Dave Letch whose guidance and expertise have been indispensable in getting the play to this point, and to Timothy Daly, who first saw the potential in this story and encouraged me to keep working on it.

Thank you to everyone at La Mama, particularly Maureen Hartley, and to Drayton Morley from Parnassus' Den for the work he puts into fostering Australian writing.

The play owes much to Joseph Frank's five volume biography of Dostoyevsky; Anna Dostoyevskaya's *Reminiscences*; David Magarshack's translation of *The Brothers Karamazov*; both the David Magarshack and the David McDuff translations of *Crime & Punishment*; the diaries of Polina Suslova; *Selected Letters of Fyodor Dostoyevsky*, edited by Joseph Frank and David I. Goldstein; and, *The Odd Man Karakozov* by Claudia Verhoeven.

Finally, thank you to all the actors who have worked on the play, especially David Pidd, Tony Sloman, Linden Wilkinson and Jonathan Hardy. Your insights and criticisms have been greatly appreciated.

CHARACTERS

FEDYA, a novelist (early–mid 40s)
ANNA, a stenographer (about 20)
KOLYA, a publisher (late 30s)
ELENA, a feminist and revolutionary (30s)
KARAKOZOV, a student revolutionary (20s)
MITYA, a soldier (late 20s–early 30s)
ALYOSHA, a novice monk (early 20s)
GRUSHENKA, Mitya's lover (30s)
KATYA, Mitya's fiancée (20s)

The parts of KOLYA/ MITYA, KARAKOZOV/ALYOSHA, ELENA/ GRUSHENKA and ANNA/KATYA should be doubled.

Other parts—LANDLADY, SOLDIER, STUDENTS, OFFICERS, etc.—are played by the Company.

The play requires a cast of five: two women and three men.

SETTING

St Petersburg, Russia, 1860s.

The set should be open and sparse, and able to accommodate a number of different settings. There may be some chairs scattered about, as well as numerous piles of books and papers. While it will overwhelmingly represent Fedya's dark and dingy flat, it needs to also serve as offices, streets, and the flats of other characters.

SCENE ONE

Darkness.

A slow, slow pounding. It starts soft, but gradually gets louder.

The pace of the pounding quickens.

OLD MAN: [*from out of the darkness*] Who's there?

> *The* OLD MAN *lights a lamp. In the glow of the lamp, we see* FEDYA. *He is lost in thought.*

Who's there?

> *Barely seen, a hand comes down violently on the* OLD MAN's *head. The blow knocks the* OLD MAN *off his feet. He loses hold of the lamp. Another blow to the* OLD MAN's *head.*

Monster! Parricide!

> *The light around the fallen lamp begins to take on a reddish tinge.*

> *More blows to the* OLD MAN's *head. The blows are fevered. Urgent. The* OLD MAN's *groans slowly subside.*

> *The noise of the blows morphs into that of a broom banging against a ceiling.*

LANDLADY: [*off*] Murder! Murder!
FEDYA: Be quiet…
LANDLADY: [*off*] Officers. Hurry—!
FEDYA: Be quiet.
LANDLADY: [*off*] Before it's me he kills—!

> *An explosion. Sudden. Distant.*

> *A second explosion.*

[*Off*] Mother of God! Mother of God!

> *A commotion somewhere outside. Voices. Whistles. All moving away from where we are.*

Then a silence—a waiting silence.

A third distant explosion.

With each explosion, the intensity of the red light has increased. It is as though FEDYA *is swimming in blood.*

Another silence.

The sound of the broom thumping.

LANDLADY: [*off*] They've bombed Apraksin market, Fyodor Mikhailovich. The students have bombed the market square.
Do you hear me?!

FEDYA: Yes.
Yes.
I hear you, yes.

The banging of the broom again.

LANDLADY: And the rent from last month, Fyodor Mikhailovich! The rent from last month. I'm still waiting for it.

Silence.

FEDYA *in a pool of red light.*

On the other side of the stage—from a distant corner of his imagination—a figure emerges. It is MITYA, *but it is impossible to see him clearly. He is just a shape in the darkness.*

MITYA: [*to* FEDYA] Who of us—tell me, brother—who of us hasn't wanted him dead?

SCENE TWO

FEDYA'S *flat. The room is darkened.*

FEDYA *is working, scribbling notes in a notebook. (This notebook should be distinctive. It should be clear that when* FEDYA *is writing in the notebook—as opposed to loose sheets of scrap paper—he is working on his story of the parricide.)*

MITYA—*the figure from his imagination—is clearly there in the room with him. He watches over* FEDYA'*s shoulder as he writes.*

MITYA: You have it wrong.
[*Pointing to the notebook*] There.
I said I wanted him dead.
I didn't say I killed him.
FEDYA: [*without looking at him*] You were jealous—
MITYA: Of my father?
FEDYA: There's a woman—
MITYA: You think I'd kill him because of her?
FEDYA: And money.
Arguments about money.
MITYA: When have there not been?
FEDYA: She led you on, this woman. Feigned that she would accept your father's proposal. Made you desperate…

FEDYA *writes.*

MITYA: Beauty's a terrible thing, brother. Mysterious and terrible all in the one moment. I look at her and want nothing more than to destroy myself. And then to have to listen to father—boasting how he keeps three thousand roubles in the house—just so he can have her…

Footsteps on the stairs.

ELENA *enters. She opens the shutters on the window, letting in a cold, blue daylight.*

MITYA *is no longer in the room.*

ELENA *kisses* FEDYA.

FEDYA: Not now.
ELENA: You're working, yes. We could hear you all the way down the stairs.
FEDYA: We?
ELENA: [*going to the door, calling through*] It's fine. He'll see us.

KARAKOZOV *enters. He fidgets. He seems nervous.*

ELENA: [*to* FEDYA] You've been killing people again, your landlady tells us.

FEDYA: Who's this?
ELENA: [*to* KARAKOZOV] Fedya likes to live out his imaginings. Don't you, Fedya? Play-act the deed before he commits it to paper.
FEDYA: I'm a curiosity for strangers, am I?
ELENA: What's it about this time, Fedya?

Another romantic triangle by the sound of it. A young man obsessed with a beautiful woman. And the old man who comes between them.

A stale sort of idea, don't you think?
FEDYA: What do you want?
ELENA: Has the young man killed the old one? Is that how it works?
FEDYA: [*referring to* KARAKOZOV] Your new pet, is he?
ELENA: It's not me who keeps the pets.

A beat.

ELENA: This is Dmitri Karakozov, Fedya.
He's a student. / Or was.
FEDYA: You were the bombs. Last night.
KARAK: Not me.
FEDYA: Your brothers then.
ELENA: He's barely been here two days. He knows nothing of the bombings.

The university in Kazan expelled him. For not paying his fees.
KARAK: It's an honour—
FEDYA: I've no money for poor students.
ELENA: He's not come here asking for money.
FEDYA: What were you studying?
KARAK: Science.
FEDYA: Science? You believe then that a man is built from the scraps of the earth—?
KARAK: No—
FEDYA: A raking together of the right measure of dirt and grease and steel—and there he is—
KARAK: No—
FEDYA: A mere engine, driven by nothing other than the cold spark of reason—
ELENA: That a man has the right to be free—that is what he believes.

FEDYA: Is there anyone who believes otherwise?
ELENA: Our Tsar—
FEDYA: Our Tsar has freed the serfs—
ELENA: To do what? To be what?
FEDYA: Perhaps they threw him out of the university because he's lacks the capacity to speak for himself.
ELENA: He dreads your answer.
FEDYA: My answer to what?
KARAK: I have a letter…
FEDYA: Of concern to me because… ?
ELENA: You have access to publishers.
FEDYA: As do you.
ELENA: I haven't your connections.

    FEDYA *holds out his hand for the letter.*

    He reads it.

KARAK: On behalf of the students of Kazan.
ELENA: On behalf of all students.
FEDYA: [*handing it back to* ELENA] Plaster it on the streets with the rest of their nonsense.
ELENA: It deserves better. You know it—
FEDYA: There is a man who waits across the alley—who opens every piece of mail before it comes through my door—who watches for me to take one wrong step—
ELENA: And informs on you so often they're still sifting through reports from years ago.
    [*To* KARAKOZOV] Tell him. Go on. What you told me.
KARAK: When they knew I was coming to Petersburg…
    There are few writers who the students respect as much as you. Because of how much you've sacrificed already.
FEDYA: I'm done with revolution. I've served my time for it.
ELENA: Yet nothing has changed.
    This is the future / of Russia, Fedya.
FEDYA: You think the beggar in the street cares about the future of Russia?
ELENA: If it means more bread in his mouth—
FEDYA: Because then he'll be happy?

ELENA: Because then he'll no longer be so distracted by hunger that he can't find the path to his own happiness.
FEDYA: In the paradise you'd build for him?
KARAK: That we will give him the means to build for himself.

A long beat.

FEDYA *puts out his hand for the letter.*

SCENE THREE

The actor playing KARAKOZOV *transitions into* ALYOSHA. *As he does so—*

[KARAKOZOV]: It's only the ordinary who must live in obedience. This is what Dostoyevsky taught me. That the extraordinary have the right—the duty—to step over the mundane obstacles of ordinary law, of entitlement… And each man's life is the proving ground. Whether he is an ordinary man—or one among the extraordinary.

The actor adds the final elements of ALYOSHA's *costume; becomes fully* ALYOSHA.

SCENE FOUR

Night. FEDYA's *flat.* FEDYA *in the shadows. He is writing (in the notebook).* MITYA *and* ALYOSHA *are with him.*

FEDYA: You'll begin not at a university, but in a monastery…?
ALYOSHA: I believe in God?
FEDYA: You believe in truth.
MITYA: Truth is whatever we can get away with.
     A woman's flesh in your hand.
FEDYA: You devote yourself to the elder there. At the monastery. Watch for him to show you the way forward. The moment when it comes.
ALYOSHA: To do what? Go where?
FEDYA: Bringing light to darkness. Your only goal. But taking a path so far from the ordinary…

Is it even possible?
ALYOSHA: What?
FEDYA: To write you. To write a thoroughly good man. A thoroughly good man whose end won't be completely misunderstood—
ALYOSHA: Why? What's to be my end?
FEDYA: Truth so far from where you ever hoped to find it.
MITYA: They told me Lazarus walking from his tomb was truth. I didn't believe it.
FEDYA: Witness it yourself. Then you'll believe.
ALYOSHA: Are you certain, brother?
    Mustn't we already believe—if we're to see the miracle when it comes?

SCENE FIVE

The noise of the roulette wheel spinning to a halt.

In a candle-lit room, we see FEDYA. *He has lost on the last spin. He searches through his pockets for more money to place. He places his last coins. The wheel spins again. He loses.*

As he plays, we see the actor transitioning from MITYA *to* KOLYA.

[KOLYA]: No-one but me at the train station, the morning he arrived back from the east.
    He'd been forgotten. He understood that. Knew his moment had passed. That there were other writers—lesser writers—who had slipped all too readily into his place.
    Ten years he was in that prison—and every day of it showed on his face, like a shadow of hell.

He is now fully KOLYA.

SCENE SIX

KOLYA's *office.* FEDYA *waits while* KOLYA *reads a letter. With an old rag,* FEDYA *dabs at a cut on his head.*

KOLYA: What happened to your head?
FEDYA: Somebody hit me. With a lump of wood.
KOLYA: Who have you upset this time?
FEDYA: It was a drunk. By Kokushkin Bridge. Lashing out at whoever passed.
KOLYA: Been to one of your dens, have you?
FEDYA: It was the only way to decide whether to give it to you or tear it up.
KOLYA: I take it you lost then.
    [*Finishes reading the letter*] It's your hand-writing, Fedya. You said it was the students' letter.
FEDYA: It needed revising.
KOLYA: Yours is the only name on it.

    A beat.

KOLYA: You're making good progress on the novel then? If you've time to be writing letters to the authorities.
FEDYA: Will you print it?
KOLYA: Why not send it to them quietly?
FEDYA: I don't want it to disappear.
KOLYA: Bombs in the middle of the city, Fedya. This is something new. Unpredictable.
FEDYA: No-one was killed. No-one was injured.
KOLYA: Livelihoods were destroyed. Peace of mind.
    Was it Elena Petrovna persuaded you to write it?
FEDYA: Shall I find another publisher?
KOLYA: Forever the gambler, Fedya. Forever certain there's no way you can lose—but lose it all you inevitably do.
FEDYA: One win is enough to counter a hundred losses.

    A beat.

KOLYA: The novel progresses well then?
FEDYA: I have no paper. Ink. The stationer—at Gostiny Dvor—he refuses to give me my order. Not until I've paid him.
KOLYA: Is the novel even started?
FEDYA: It can't be done. / It's impossible.
KOLYA: It must be done. / You have a contract—
FEDYA: I have other things—important things—
KOLYA: [*referring to the letter*] Like this?
FEDYA: Ideas. Pages and pages of them.
About a man who murders his father.
KOLYA: Then write it and send it to Stellovsky.
FEDYA: I wouldn't waste it on a crook like him.
KOLYA: You signed his contract. You took his money.
FEDYA: I won't rush out another half-baked novel just to satisfy him—
KOLYA: You write this novel or he owns you—
FEDYA: I won't give him this story—
KOLYA: Then throw something together. Anything.
FEDYA: How?
KOLYA: I don't know.
I don't know.
WE'LL find an answer, Fedya. We always have, you and I.
[*Holding out money*] For the stationer.
FEDYA: And the letter?
KOLYA: I'll put it to the censorship committee.
Must it be under your name?
FEDYA: There's not a word there I fear.
KOLYA: Under ordinary circumstances, perhaps not. But these are no longer ordinary circumstances.

A beat.

KOLYA *gestures towards the money again.* FEDYA *takes it.*

SCENE SEVEN

The street outside a coffee house. KARAKOZOV *is distributing leaflets.*

STUDENT/S: [*off*] We have no need of a power that persecutes its people—a power that thwarts the development of our nation. We have no need of a power that raises corruption and self-seeking as its banner. Let the words of the people—the deeds of the people—be its end. Whatever the cost, so must it be.

During this, ANNA *arrives. She is looking around, trying to find the place she is meant to be.*

At the sound of a whistle, KARAKOZOV *hurries away. As he does so, he pushes a leaflet into* ANNA's *hands. She is looking at it when* KOLYA *approaches.*

KOLYA: [*referring to the leaflet*] Yours?
ANNA: No.
    No.
    I don't understand it. All this hate.
KOLYA: You've taken the words from my mouth.
ANNA: You're Nikolai Ivanovich?
KOLYA: And you're Anna. But you must call me Kolya.
    Come inside. I'll order us coffee.

As they move inside, KOLYA *gestures for two coffees. They sit.*

During the following, coffee and cakes etc are served.

KOLYA: [*handing her a note*] Stolyarney Lane—house of Alonkin—apartment 13. Ask for Dostoyevsky.
ANNA: Fyodor Mikhailovich Dostoyevsky?
KOLYA: Your professor didn't tell you?
ANNA: No…
KOLYA: I need someone who knows his work—
ANNA: I know his work, yes—
KOLYA: The importance of what he does—
ANNA: I understand—

KOLYA: I'm sure you do—
ANNA: But Nikolai Ivanovich—
KOLYA: Kolya.
ANNA: Kolya—
   The novelist Dostoyevsky?
KOLYA: He's nothing to be afraid of. Believe me.
   Your professor said you were top of your class.
ANNA: I was.
KOLYA: Then you're already cleverer than Fedya.
   Work hard—and keep working him hard—and all of Russia will be in your debt.
   [*Indicating the note*] The directions are there. And a small down-payment. To get you started.

He offers her a cake/pastry. She hesitates, then takes one.

KOLYA: Yes. We have each other's trust. I feel it.
   Together, Anna, we will see this done.

SCENE EIGHT

FEDYA*'s door.* ANNA *knocks. Waits. Listens, her ear close to the door. Knocks again.*

LANDLADY: [*off*] He's not there.
ANNA: I was told to keep knocking. That he pretends not to hear.
LANDLADY: [*off*] He's never there this time of day.
ANNA: I heard voices. Inside.
LANDLADY: [*off*] Then you want to stay well clear. He's a madman. Would cut your throat as soon as look at you.
ANNA: You're mistaken, I'm sure—
LANDLADY: [*off*] He has no money. He won't be able to pay you. No matter what services you're offering.
ANNA: I'm not—
   He's not—
   I'm a stenographer.
LANDLADY: [*off*] Whatever it is you're calling yourself nowadays, he's not worth the effort. Not even for a mountain of gold.

SCENE NINE

FEDYA's *flat. It is dark. The faint sound of knocking.*

FEDYA *is working;* MITYA *and* ALYOSHA *are with him.*

MITYA: He's turned you against me.
ALYOSHA: No.
MITYA: You're always hurrying away.
ALYOSHA: Listening to you reminds me what I am.
MITYA: What's that?
ALYOSHA: The same as you.
MITYA: You and me? The same?
ALYOSHA: We share the same blood, the same history. Why not the same future?

Knocking.

MITYA: You know she has her eye on you. My woman.
   Says all you need is the fury of a lover's touch and you'd be cured.
ALYOSHA: Cured?
MITYA: Of your obscene dedication to the truth.
   Keep your distance, brother. She'll test you like she's tested the rest of us.
ALYOSHA: Stay away from father.
MITYA: Let him take everything that's mine—?
ALYOSHA: He is playing us one against the other—
MITYA: The hate that's in my heart—
ALYOSHA: I'm scared what you'll do.

A beat.

FEDYA: [*to himself; barely heard*] If we could discard God…
MITYA: [*to* FEDYA] You think I don't hear you muttering? You think it doesn't make perfect sense?
ALYOSHA: What? What does he say?

Knocking.

MITYA: [*to* FEDYA] Tell him.

>*A beat.*

Always quiet as the grave…

[*To* ALYOSHA] All we need do is let go of this absurd hope that there's something more—something beyond us—and we'd know it.
[*To* FEDYA] Isn't that right, brother?
ALYOSHA: Know what?
MITYA: Nothing is sinful.

>*Knocking.*

ALYOSHA: What does he know/ of sin—?
MITYA: Anything—everything—is allowed.

>*Knocking.*

FEDYA: To kill a thing as foul and sordid as our father…?
MITYA: Under such a system, it'd almost be an obligation.

>*Insistent knocking.*

SCENE TEN

ANNA *at* FEDYA*'s door. She is knocking.*

As she's knocking, FEDYA *opens the door in a rush.*

FEDYA: What?

>ANNA *is dumb-struck.*

What?

>ANNA *grasps at words.*

FEDYA: Go away.
ANNA: I was sent—
FEDYA: I don't care.
ANNA: I was sent you're expecting me.
FEDYA: I'm not—
ANNA: For the novel—
FEDYA: The novel—?
ANNA: There's a deadline and he gave/ me—

FEDYA: He sent you?
ANNA: This address and/ I'm here and I'm to—
FEDYA: You tell Stellovsky, Miss—
ANNA: I don't know who you think—
FEDYA: Tell him he can threaten me all he wants—
ANNA: I don't know anyone called Stellovsky —
FEDYA: There is no novel, there will be no novel—
ANNA: I'm the stenographer—

>FEDYA *slams the door shut.*

[*Through the door*] I'm the stenographer!

>*A beat.*

>FEDYA *opens the door again.*

Nikolai Ivanovich sent me.

>*A beat.*

>FEDYA *moves into the flat, leaving the door open.* ANNA *realises she's expected to follow.*

>*Inside, the room is still quite dark.* FEDYA *sits himself down and picks up his pen. His hand hovers over his notebook.*

>*A silence.*

[*Filling the silence*] That you weren't here. That's what I thought. At first. Or not answering. The number of times I knocked. I'd have gone. Given up. But Kolya— [*Correcting herself*] Nikolai Ivanovich—he said if you didn't answer—

>FEDYA *gestures for her to be quiet.*

>*Silence.*

[*Again needing to fill the silence*] Your landlady, she said you were dangerous. That you wouldn't be here. That you're never here. She said to go home. But I could hear you talking and—

>*Another gesture to be quiet.*

>*A beat.*

THE PARRICIDE

FEDYA *returns to the notebook. His hand hovering again, as though ready to write. After a moment, he gives it up. He goes about the room, opening shutters etc, letting in light.*

FEDYA: A universe of ideas and what do I have to show for it? Half a page of nonsense. Sentences barely breathing. Because you knock at my door.

ANNA: I could go—

FEDYA: Too late—

ANNA: Come back—

FEDYA: It's dead now.

Your name again?

ANNA: Anna Grigorevna.

FEDYA: I had a dream last night, Anna Grigorevna. A flea biting at me as I slept. I pulled my mattress apart searching for it, but it wouldn't be found. So on it went. Biting and biting. Was that you, do you think?

ANNA: A dream is a dream.

FEDYA: Is that meant to be a clever answer?

ANNA: No.

FEDYA: You're looking at my eye.

ANNA: No.

FEDYA: You are.

ANNA: I'm not.

FEDYA: You think it odd.

ANNA: No.

FEDYA: Why not? It is odd.

A fit. Last night. I fell. Knocked my eye. See? It seems I have no iris at all.

He is very close to her.

FEDYA: Kolya's told you you'd be working for an ex-convict?

ANNA: Your sentence is finished, sir.

FEDYA: But you're never entirely free.

Do you know why I was imprisoned?

ANNA: Yes.

FEDYA: I'm not a murderer, no matter what my landlady thinks.

ANNA: No.

FEDYA: I spoke my mind.
　　Nothing for you to fear.
　　A beat.
There must be a scrap of some abandoned novel here somewhere. Something worthless enough for Stellovsky...

> FEDYA *begins searching among his papers. Realising he's not going to clear a space for her,* ANNA *finds herself somewhere to sit, takes her notepad etc from her case.*
>
> FEDYA *has gathered together what seem like scraps of paper— bits of this and that, of various sizes. He has a handful of them. He starts organising them into some sort of order, finds the one that he'll begin with. The whole business is quite involved and time-consuming.*
>
> *He seems about to begin. Hesitates.*

[*Conversationally*] Do you want tea?
ANNA: No.
FEDYA: Brandy?
ANNA: No.
FEDYA: The landlady used to bring me tea. When she knew I was here. Every other hour, a whole new pot. Even soup sometimes. Cake if she was feeling particularly generous. Until the incident with the rock. She thought I was going to kill her. I wasn't. I was just working, but—. She hasn't brought me so much as a mouthful of tea since. 'If it's in your head. If it's in your head to do it,' she says, 'then who's to say that your hands won't one day follow?'
　　A beat.
FEDYA: You know my writing?
ANNA: A little.
FEDYA: *Crime and Punishment.* My last novel. You must know it.
ANNA: The work, sir.
FEDYA: Just say. If you haven't read it.
　　I don't bite.
ANNA: I haven't read it.
FEDYA: There. Not so difficult.

Why haven't you read it?
ANNA: I—I've not had the time.
FEDYA: Why, what have you been doing?
ANNA: Studying.
FEDYA: You're a student?
ANNA: I was.
FEDYA: Of what?
ANNA: Stenography.
FEDYA: Yes. A student. Of stenography.
 Where did you study?
ANNA: Where did I study?
FEDYA: Where did you study?
ANNA: Does it matter?
FEDYA: Some institutions have better reputations than others.
ANNA: For stenography?
FEDYA: For unrest.
ANNA: You're asking if I'm a revolutionary?
FEDYA: Are you?
ANNA: Not all students are revolutionaries.
FEDYA: Are you?
ANNA: No.
FEDYA: There weren't mumblings of sedition amongst your fellow students?
ANNA: You think there's a cabal of stenographers plotting to overthrow the Tsar?
FEDYA: What do I know of stenographers and their persuasions?
ANNA: Is there to be any work/ at all this morning—?
FEDYA: Why didn't you have the time? To read my book.
ANNA: I told you. I was studying.
FEDYA: The rest of Petersburg seems to have had the time.
 Is stenography so arduous a course—?
ANNA: I was caring for my dying father.
 I was caring for my father.

  A long beat.

FEDYA: Have you been asked to reveal what I'm writing?
ANNA: By whom?

FEDYA: By anyone. By Kolya.
ANNA: No.
FEDYA: What notes I make?
ANNA: No.
FEDYA: Where I go? Who I see?
ANNA: Do you need watching?
FEDYA: There are people who seem to think so. You'd be surprised the sort of people hired to do the watching.
 What's your relationship with Kolya?
ANNA: My relationship?
FEDYA: Why did he send you?
ANNA: He said I'd be helping a famous novelist—
FEDYA: That's what he told you to tell me?
ANNA: I had hoped it might be Tolstoy.
FEDYA: Have you read any of my work?
ANNA: Some.
FEDYA: And?
 And?
ANNA: It was a little too sentimental for my taste.

A beat.

FEDYA: You can go.
 It won't work.
 There's. No. Job.

SCENE ELEVEN

KOLYA*'s office.* ANNA *puts money on the table.*

ANNA: He said there's no job. No novel.
KOLYA: No novel?
ANNA: That's what he said.
KOLYA: How was he? How did he seem?
ANNA: How did he seem?
KOLYA: Anxious? Troubled?
ANNA: Rude. Hateful.
 Old.

KOLYA: You need to go back.
ANNA: He doesn't seem to like you very much.
KOLYA: I know.
ANNA: You said you were friends.
KOLYA: We're Russian friends. Bound together by a mutual hatred.
Give me one day. Then try him again.
One day.
[*Pushing the money back towards her*] For your trouble so far.
She leaves without taking the money.

SCENE TWELVE

The actor playing ANNA *transitions into* KATYA. *As she does—*

[ANNA]: I'd read *Crime and Punishment*—of course I'd read it. I'd read every book he'd ever written. But if he thought I was going to give him the satisfaction...

I'd read it each day as I walked to and from the institute. And then, at night, I'd read it again to my father. It was a heavy presence all through Petersburg, that book—and my father wouldn't be denied it.

Late at night, as he waited for sleep, my father would tell me the dark story of Dostoyevsky's arrest. His imprisonment. And the tears would well in my father's eyes. This, he said—this is how Russia treats her saviours. And it broke my heart to hear it.

SCENE THIRTEEN

A candle-lit room. A roulette wheel spinning. FEDYA *stands watching the wheel spin and stop, spin and stop. He is barely aware of what is happening with the wheel—he's absorbed by the figures in his imagination—*MITYA *and* KATYA.

MITYA: I didn't think you'd come.
Are things so desperate?

A beat.

MITYA: I can't help you if you won't speak.
KATYA: My father is dying.
MITYA: That much I know.
KATYA: He has debts. If he dies before they are paid…
MITYA: He dies shamed.
KATYA: It's not himself he's worried for. It's my mother, his children.
MITYA: It's a lot of money.
KATYA: If you hadn't said you'd loan it to him…
MITYA: The loan would not be to your father.

A beat.

This is a matter of business.
A loan at a judicious rate.
Some gift would need to be given in return…
VOICE: [*off*] Place your money.

FEDYA'*s attention is brought back to the roulette wheel.* KATYA *and* MITYA *recede into the darkness.*

FEDYA *watches the wheel spin. He places his money.*

SCENE FOURTEEN

MITYA *transitions back into* KOLYA.

[KOLYA]: It's its own myth, that morning in Semyonovsky square. That morning he was slated to die, paraded on the scaffold with the other criminals. A story that cascaded, man to man to man, through the cells where I was still being held, and each of us awaiting a similar fate…

We'd met first at Petrashevsky's meetings, his circle of like-minded thinkers—and Fedya like an apparition on its edges—absorbing every word—but biding his time—holding close his opinions…

And when he did at last speak… I can still hear him. The way his voice blazed out from him…

All of us there—testing ideas—moving towards a singular vision of the future… All of us condemned for it.

Just as the rifles were aiming towards the prisoners, the Tsar intervened.

Fedya was sent to Siberia.

A different category of death…

SCENE FIFTEEN

FEDYA's *flat.* KOLYA *is happily ensconced when* FEDYA *enters.* FEDYA *goes about the room, closing up notebooks, hiding papers.*

FEDYA: I've told the landlady not to let you in.

KOLYA: She's easily charmed.

FEDYA: The roubles you throw at her don't hurt.

A beat.

KOLYA: No novel?

I send you the answer to your prayers and you tell her there's no novel.

FEDYA: Tell who?

KOLYA: Anna.

Young. Pretty. Brown hair… Ahh. He remembers.

This novel will be written, Fedya, if I have to write it for you myself.

Unless Stellovsky is satisfied with whatever you throw his way, I get no new work from you. Not a word. He'll have everything. For the next eight years. You'll get not one kopek. And I'll be publishing one blank page after another. How then am I to help you?

A long beat.

FEDYA: Send her if you must.

KOLYA: I'll tell her to come tomorrow.

FEDYA: Just keep away from her. Until the book is finished. Pursue her then.

A beat.

How's your wife?

KOLYA: Happily languishing on her father's estate.

It's a matter of understanding the boundaries, Fedya. What can and cannot be crossed.

FEDYA: Did you send my letter to the committee?

KOLYA: You'd put your own life on the line to support some ragtag students?

The Tsar liberalised the universities. Called back all those who'd been banished under his father. Made provision so that the poor could attend—

FEDYA: All rescinded—

KOLYA: Because they've decided they'd rather turn themselves into powder kegs and blow Russia apart at the first opportunity.

FEDYA: They need a keener hand to guide them. That's all. Someone who'll steer them away from all this talk of destruction—

KOLYA: You're thinking you?

FEDYA: Some sway in the order of things. A voice—

KOLYA: We're to let them loose in government now? Keep extending political rights to those who've no idea what to do with them—?

FEDYA: There is in your thinking a defect that I both hate and despise.

KOLYA: Until you need my money.

We were on the same side of this once.

FEDYA: Were we?

KOLYA: You know we were.

Determined to break the power of the censors, no matter what. Pushing for the freedom of the serfs—

FEDYA: This is the history you cling to—?

KOLYA: Proof that change can come—will come—but in its time—

FEDYA: Because I don't remember it, Kolya. You standing beside me on the scaffold while I waited my turn/ to die—

KOLYA: What chance did I have? Chained up/ in their stinking hole—

FEDYA: If I knew the students who planted the bombs, I'd not name them.

No matter the circumstances.

I would not name them.

A long beat.

KOLYA: Write your book, Fedya. Let that be the hand that guides Russia forward.

FEDYA *busies himself with his papers.*

KOLYA *exits.*

A beat.

FEDYA *takes his coat. Exits to the street. Tears a flyer from the doorpost as he passes.*

The sound of a roulette wheel.

SCENE SIXTEEN

The sound of the wheel morphs into the steady rhythm of a printing press. KARAKOZOV *in a dark room working the presses. There are others there with him, but he is the only one we see.*

STUDENT/S [*off*] We will be committed.
    We will have no interests of our own.
    No relations.
    No attachments.
    No possessions.
    No name.
    Everything in us immersed in this one singular passion…

SCENE SEVENTEEN

FEDYA *and* ANNA *working. As* ANNA *takes dictation,* FEDYA *juggles all his scraps of papers, getting them in the right order. He is energised—barely stops for breath.* ANNA *struggles to keep up.*

FEDYA: [*dictating*] … and, by some strange perversity, I made a point of putting all my money on it, taking mad risks, a terrible craving to dare possessing me. The sensation that gripped my soul, not killing my desire, no, but feeding it, stirring it, stronger and stronger, until my spirit was entirely spent, until there was nothing left of the man I knew myself to be, of the man—

ANNA: Slower!

FEDYA: Slower?

ANNA: If you have any pity.

My hand's beginning to ache. After a whole morning at such a pace.

FEDYA: How much have we done?

ANNA: Twenty pages at least.

FEDYA: This will work.

This will work.

I can see light—I think it's light—at the end of the tunnel.

ANNA *subtly tries to work the ache from her hand.*

Here. Give me your hand.

ANNA *tentatively holds out her hand. He begins to massage it.*

ANNA: [*quickly drawing her hand away*] That's not necessary.

FEDYA: [*taking her hand again*] On a good day, when the ideas take hold of me, wrestle me into submission—good days that have become rarer and rarer—I need to work my own hand like this.

A beat.

It was taught to me by one of the prisoners in the camp.

He was a blacksmith. In the Engineers. The Army. Before he was jailed. He killed his father. In a jealous rage, but that's not… His hands would cramp, particularly in the cold weather. And he would sit hour after hour kneading the rigidity from them. I used to marvel at the strength of them. His hands. Until I understood what he'd done with them.

It's a good story for a novel, don't you think? A man who kills his father?

ANNA: You should write it.

FEDYA: I will. I am. The ideas are here—in the shadows. They're just waiting for me to yield to them.

A long beat.

ANNA: What was it like there?

In the prison camps?

FEDYA: You're watched. Relentlessly. Not alone for a single minute and you… you come to hate mankind. So many souls packed into such a small space. And what's yours—what's left to you—you hold to yourself like a shining prize. Your thoughts—they're all you have. And when they're precisely what's condemned you...

But I never knew myself so well as when I was there.

A disturbance from downstairs. The LANDLADY *trying to stop someone from coming up the stairs.*

ANNA *pulls her hand away and stands on the other side of the room, gathering papers etc, as* ELENA *enters.*

ELENA *is oblivious to* ANNA.

ELENA: Your guard-dog is a very tenacious today, Fedya. [*Noticing* ANNA] Aah. She obviously felt you weren't to be disturbed.

FEDYA: Anna is the stenographer.

ELENA: Not quite what you described.

A change, at least, from the sickly virgins who usually moon after you. But isn't she a poppet? Now I look at her more closely. But aren't you a darling, with your cheeks all ablaze? And such pretty, pretty eyes. Aren't they, Fedya? Surely you've noticed the lovely brown of her eyes.

FEDYA: What do I care the colour of her eyes? What do you want?

ELENA: Send her away.

FEDYA: We're working.

ELENA: I was working last night—it didn't stop you storming in—

FEDYA: I'd have turned right around—

ELENA: Once you'd done with me—

FEDYA: It was you who started it—

ELENA: Refusing to leave till you'd gone through every page, looking out for your name—

FEDYA: Then find someone other than me to write about.

ELENA: You think I haven't anything better to write about than you? I wouldn't set my ambitions so low.

FEDYA: What do you want?

ELENA: I need a reason to be here now?

FEDYA: We're working.

ELENA: Whatever you want to call it.

FEDYA: Why are you here plaguing my life?

ELENA: You think I want this misery again?

FEDYA: Then go—
ELENA: On your knees you said you were—
FEDYA: You think I'd shed a tear/ if you walked out—?
ELENA: Swore you'd die without me—
FEDYA: Better dead than this—
ELENA: You destroy/ my life—
FEDYA: You crush/ my will—
ELENA: If I asked you to kill a man...
 If I asked you to kill a man, would you do it?
FEDYA: Which man?
ELENA: Any man I choose.
FEDYA: Yes. Right now, yes.

 A beat.

ELENA: [*to* ANNA] You can go.
ANNA: But the work—
FEDYA: Go. There'll be no more work today.

 ANNA *realises there is no point arguing further. She exits.*

 A beat.

 ELENA *sits.*

 A beat.

 FEDYA *falls at her feet, kisses her stockings etc.*

SCENE EIGHTEEN

The actor playing ELENA *transtions into* GRUSHENKA. *As she does so—*

[ELENA]: He was a difficult man to say No to, when the fire was in his eyes. The fierceness...
 I knew it the first time we loved. In the grass it was. On the edge of the park at Lublino...
 Within a week he'd worked me loose of my marriage and there was no going back. Not to my life as it had been...
 Until his wife called him back to her—plucked at his guilt with her whining and ailing.

I thought I would die… thought I was dead… but…

There was a young man in our village. Went off to study the law. Came back certain of nothing but that it must be dragged down. And the Tsar and his nobles with it… He filled entirely the void Fedya had created in me—gave me my voice—teased out from me what I had for so long yearned to say…

It was when tuberculosis took him that I could think of nothing else but finding Fedya again.

She is now fully GRUSHENKA.

SCENE NINETEEN

We see FEDYA. *He is writing in his notebook.* GRUSHENKA *is present in his imagination.*

We see MITYA *and* KATYA, *just as they were in scene thirteen.*

MITYA: The loan would not be to your father.

> *A beat.*
>
> This is a matter of business.
> A loan at a judicious rate.
> Some gift would need to be given in return.

KATYA: I understand.

> *As* GRUSHENKA *speaks,* MITYA *approaches* KATYA, *begins caressing her face. Lets his hands run lightly over her body. He is clearly planning to take her.*

GRUSHENKA: [*to* FEDYA] I know you think you love her.

> I see the way you watch her.

FEDYA: Why play him off against his father? If you love him so much?

GRUSHENKA: To discover how much I love him. Is that answer enough for you? To discover how much he loves me.

> Or maybe because it's what women do.
>
> *A beat.*

You've no need to pine over them. He won't have her. He hasn't the nerve. Not for this. Not for murder.

You know what must be done. Know in your heart he's not the man to do it.
FEDYA: He said he'd kill him—
GRUSHENKA: He's all bluster and air—
FEDYA: He wants his father dead—
GRUSHENKA: Not as fiercely as you do.

Oh, you have your reconciliation. You drink your father's wine and tell him stories and pretend you don't hate him—pretend you've forgotten the past...

He will bungle the deed and then weep when it's done.

No, what you need is a brave man. A man who dares...
MITYA: [*stepping back fom* KATYA] You can go.
KATYA: But the money?
MITYA: It's yours.
KATYA: But I have no way to...
MITYA: Go.
GRUSHENKA: There. You see?

All bluster and air.

SCENE TWENTY

Night. Pounding of the printing presses.

KARAKOZOV *is nailing flyers to the walls and gates of houses.*

STUDENT/S: [*off*] All our resources—all our energy—must be directed towards increasing—intensifying—the miseries that people suffer.
And we will go on doing so.
Until their patience is exhausted.
Until the people are driven to rise against their oppressors.

The pounding of the printing press fades, bleeding into the next scene.

SCENE TWENTY-ONE

FEDYA's *flat*. FEDYA *is sleeping, notes and work scattered around him. A single bang that might be the sound of a gunshot wakes him. A second banging sound (it could be a gunshot; it could be the broomstick).*

LANDLADY: [*off*] Fyodor Mikhailovich!

> *The pounding of the* LANDLADY's *broomstick.*

> The Magistrate from the fourth district. The one who put that revolutionary away. Shot in his carriage.
> Do you hear me, Fyodor Mikhailovich?! Who among us will be spared?

> *Low sound of a roulette wheel slowly spinning.*

> *It spins faster. Louder.*

SCENE TWENTY-TWO

FEDYA's *flat.* ANNA *waiting. Eventually,* FEDYA *arrives bearing pastries etc. He empties the pockets of his coat as he takes it off, throws handfuls of coins on the table. There is something almost manic about him.*

FEDYA: What time did you get here?
ANNA: An hour ago.
FEDYA: You were due at 10.
ANNA: The roads were barricaded. The cab needed to find another way.
FEDYA: You were due at 10.
ANNA: We're working today then, are we?
FEDYA: There. Pastries. From the bakery on Kremensky. Nothing cheers a woman more than stuffing her face with something sweet. [*Going to the door; yelling to the* LANDLADY *downstairs*] What chance is there of some tea, Agafya Pavlovich?
LANDLADY: [*off*] For you? None.
FEDYA: [*to* ANNA] Go downstairs and get some tea from her.
LANDLADY: [*off*] I'm still waiting on last month's rent.

FEDYA: [*gesturing to the money on the table*] And take her a handful of that to shut her up.
ANNA: I'm not here to make your tea. Nor to pay your rent.
FEDYA: Where are the pages from yesterday?

> ANNA *retrieves them and hands them over.*

You can go.

> ANNA *doesn't move.*

You can go!
ANNA: You have a contract—
FEDYA: It bleeds me dry—
ANNA: Stellovsky will own you—
FEDYA: Do you think I care?

I have this. [*Gesturing to his notebook*] This is all I need. All I am.
ANNA: One week and it's done. You're free. We both are.
FEDYA: Do you understand the ocean of debt I'm drowning in—?
ANNA: Then meet your contract—
FEDYA: That only last week my crazed sister-in-law was back here demanding I buy her son out of the military/ because it no longer suits him?
ANNA: And there it is. Today's great woe—
FEDYA: You think I don't want to clear my debts? Be a free man again—?
ANNA: Any excuse. Any distraction. And you chase it like a dog after its tail. This novel won't be written while you're forever searching for the next thing to suffer over.

I don't understand it. This misery you cling to.
FEDYA: It's my lucky charm. It keeps me alive.
ANNA: It's a vanity.
FEDYA: Do you know where I've been?
ANNA: Gambling.
FEDYA: Gambling, yes. With my life. With the future…

I see it now, Anna. Where to place my money. Where I'd been so fearful of placing it. They are right. The students. To a point, they are right. What must be done…What it is our right, our duty…

> *A slow tapping sound, building. A slow pounding.*

FEDYA *stares into the middle-distance, the almost trance-like state that precedes a fit.*

ANNA *realises something is wrong.*

ANNA: Fyodor Mikhailovich—

The lights dim.

Fyodor Mikhailovich—

The room is in shadows.

Reality gives way to FEDYA*'s imagination.*

FEDYA *and* ALYOSHA *are lit by an incredibly white light.*

ALYOSHA *is on his knees.*

FEDYA: Off your knees.
You've no need to mourn.
ALYOSHA: He's dead.
FEDYA: I know.
ALYOSHA: My teacher.
FEDYA: Another will come.
ALYOSHA: I want no other.
FEDYA: This is not your path.
ALYOSHA: His body's fallen to dust.
FEDYA: As any man's.
ALYOSHA: I believed him more than a man.
FEDYA: You must abandon him.
ALYOSHA: It has hardened me—
FEDYA: Yes.
ALYOSHA: Hardened my faith.
FEDYA: No, no, the miracle didn't come.
ALYOSHA: That I am on my knees. That I have seen my way. Is that not miracle enough?
FEDYA: There's no truth to be found here. Not in abject service to prayer and ritual. To venal laws. That's what you will come to understand.
ALYOSHA: I understand all I need to understand. Have seen here—on my knees—all I need to see.
That there is only one doorway to perfection and that is death.

That demand all you want your heaven here on earth, you can never have it.

That you, brother—you're just as scared as the rest of us.

A shift in the light. ALYOSHA *recedes into the shadows as* FEDYA *suffers a fit.*

ANNA *can do nothing but watch.*

SCENE TWENTY-THREE

FEDYA's *flat.* ELENA *sits reading through the pages of a manuscript.* KOLYA *enters.*

KOLYA: How is he?
ELENA: He's sleeping.
KOLYA: Anna said it was bad.
ELENA: No worse, I expect, than usual.
KOLYA: Were you here?
ELENA: Anna hasn't already told you?
KOLYA: Would I be asking if she had?
ELENA: The landlady's girl fetched me.
KOLYA: You know what's brought it on.
ELENA: Do I?
KOLYA: Letters defending the students?
　　He'll not be your propagandist.
ELENA: You think the money you keep feeding him will one day make him yours?
KOLYA: He has friends who'll ensure he travels no further down that road than he already has.
ELENA: He's not forgotten, Nikolai Ivanovich—he's been betrayed before, when he believed himself among friends.

　　FEDYA *emerges. He is weak.*

FEDYA: Here we all are. Together again.

He sits at his work table, stares at it as though he wants to do something, but lacks the wherewithal to begin.

FEDYA: But you were talking. Don't let me stop you.
   An argument. About my future. My intentions.
KOLYA: It's all moved too fast, Fedya. The risks now far outweigh any good you can do—
ELENA: Better to do nothing then—to stand up bravely for the status quo—

   During the following ANNA *enters. Her arrival is barely acknowledged.*

KOLYA: Support the students and you give your name to every madness they enact. You might as well hold the gun yourself.
ELENA: It's a risk worth taking—
KOLYA: Easy to say when it's not your liberty at stake—
ELENA: It's precisely my liberty at stake—
ANNA: Do you hear yourselves?
   Can you not understand what you're doing to him?
ELENA: Get out. Both of you.
FEDYA: You say you want a book from me, Kolya?
KOLYA: Your first contract after Stellovsky's is done.
FEDYA: How about this? A man at a crossroads. Three possible ways before him. Pilgrim. Revolutionary. Or husband. Which does he choose? Which would you have him choose? What'll get me the most money?
KOLYA: You cater your writing to the buyer now?
FEDYA: It's what I'm known as, isn't it? A hack?
KOLYA: I thought *Crime and Punishment* changed all that.
FEDYA: Yet here I am, still expected to churn out novels under the threat of a stick.
KOLYA: They all come with their own risk. It'd depend on what he intends to wager, this hero of yours.
FEDYA: Not on how much he might win?
KOLYA: Is he likely to win?
FEDYA: What do you say, Anna? Which road is my hero's way to happiness?

   A beat.

FEDYA: Which road?
ANNA: Husband.

FEDYA: No doubt?

ANNA: None. If those are his choices…

FEDYA: Should he seek then an intelligent companion, or merely a kind one?

ANNA: [*deferring to* ELENA] An intelligent one.

FEDYA: I think he should choose a kind one. So she'll take pity on him and love him.

ELENA: Have you done with your love play, Fedya? Shame on you, to turn a young girl's head so cruelly. You know which road you must take. You know where/ you should be—

FEDYA: They've offered me a fine choice, Anna. The terror of revolution or the terror of the state—our lives balanced on whether we set our bet on the red or the black.

What is it? Tell me. That one thing that will push a man full over the edge. Not teetering at its brink, but…

ELENA: You should rest now, Fedya.

FEDYA: We have work to do. Anna and I.

ELENA: Leave it for another day.

KOLYA: She's right,/ Fedya.

FEDYA: You want me to work. Let me work.

A beat.

KOLYA *leaves.*

ELENA *waits.*

FEDYA *makes it clear he expects her to go also.*

A beat.

ELENA *exits.*

ANNA *readies herself for work.* FEDYA *struggles for something to say.*

FEDYA: It's still dark…

There's a place I go, Anna—before the fit overtakes me—a place of such transparency… I'd give my whole life to stay there for one moment longer…

A beat.

I have in my mind such a tale. A story that is everything I need to say. Of a parricide.

ANNA: You've told me.

FEDYA: I have?

ANNA: A little.

FEDYA: A mystery. Which of the father's two sons was it who killed him? But they refuse to do my bidding. The sons. Refuse to act as I would have them act.

ANNA: Perhaps they know best.

FEDYA: Know more than me? Yes. Yes, perhaps they do. Only…

There seems to me now to be a third son—it becomes clearer and clearer to me—but I don't know who he is—not yet. I don't understand him—but he won't let go of me—

My mind is filled day and night with nothing else—and whenever I seem on the verge of understanding, this piece of nothing I'm writing for Stellovsky pushes itself into my brain…

Minutes ago, when I walked into this room, it seemed to me to be teeming with life. Now it seems like nothing so much as a tomb—and all I want to do is run from it.

ANNA: Finish the little of Stellovsky's book that is left to finish, then there'll be nothing to do but write your parricide.

FEDYA: Will you help me? Will you stay?

ANNA: One book at a time, Fyodor Mikhailovich.

FEDYA: How many pages have we done?

ANNA: One hundred and sixteen.

FEDYA: Thirty-four to go.

ANNA: You write your books by the page?

FEDYA: If it's what I'm paid by.

ANNA: You stop when you've reached the required number?

FEDYA: I see it looming and wrap things up as quickly as I can.

ANNA: I was beginning to wonder if you knew how to smile.

FEDYA: I even know how to laugh.

A beat.

FEDYA: Have you ever been in love?

ANNA: Is this another effort to laugh? Asking me about my love life?

FEDYA: Here's something would make anyone laugh. I proposed to three women. After my wife died. None of whom, I see now, I actually loved. And all of whom said, No.

ANNA: What does it say about you, Fyodor Mikhailovich? Endless contracts and marriage proposals. Determined to lock yourself into one or the other.

FEDYA: I don't know. What does it say about me?

ANNA: Sign no more contracts—and find yourself a woman who'll love you—else you'll do no more with your great book than flirt at its edges.

FEDYA: Have you ever been in love?

ANNA: I'm not sure that's any of your/ business—

FEDYA: Have you ever been in love?

ANNA: When I was sixteen I was in love with the hero of a novel. Will that do you?

FEDYA: The hero of a novel? Well... what mortal man could hope to compete.

A long beat.

FEDYA: Some days, Anna—some days I feel I am the blackest of rebels...

I've had meetings with the students—

ANNA: Don't,/ Fyodor Mikhailovich—

FEDYA: Have read their treatises and felt so sharp a desire...

There is something that was never known—never discovered...

Years ago. Before my arrest. I was involved in another group. A more secret group—

ANNA: Don't—

FEDYA: Our sole aim was to provoke revolution—absolute revolution—in order to see the serfs freed. We'd have stopped at nothing. So dark was our anger. Had it been discovered then, I'd have been shot. Not a question asked. Even now, were it ever/ discovered—

ANNA: Please, Fyodor Mikhailovich. No more.

You should rest. You should rest.

I'll go downstairs.

I'll get you tea.

ANNA *hurries away.*

The shadows close in on FEDYA. *He sees* ALYOSHA.

As FEDYA *speaks,* ALYOSHA *transtions into* KARAKOZOV.

FEDYA: I must have retribution or I will destroy myself.

Why must it come only in some infinity of space and time? Why? I want to see it with my own eyes. The lion lie down with the lamb. The murdered man rise up to embrace his murderer. I want to be there when it's finally revealed. What all the suffering has been for.

I don't want to shake your faith. I don't. I want you to shake mine. I beg you to…

A series of explosions.

The urgent banging of a broom-head from the floor below.

SCENE TWENTY-FOUR

KARAKOZOV'*s room.*

FEDYA *and* KARAKOZOV.

FEDYA: Who's making these decisions?
KARAK: No-one.
FEDYA: Tell me. Let me speak/ to them.
KARAK: We have no leaders. We have no need of leaders. We're equal—each of us finding our own way to bring the ideas/ to their proper conclusion.
FEDYA: Until you've destroyed everything. Then you'll see how many leaders you have, all of them rushing over each other to step into the vacuum they've created.
KARAK: I don't know who bombed the palace. I don't.
   I know it wasn't me.
   But if it had been?
   If it had been my hand that lit the fuse?
   Wouldn't I have had just cause?
FEDYA: No—
KARAK: Wouldn't you have had just cause, Fyodor Mikhailovich? Given what you suffered at the Tsar's hands—?

FEDYA: It was a different Tsar. A different time—
KARAK: But the same system.
　　Men condemned to death. For saying what they think.
FEDYA: Everything will be lost.
KARAK: Then there was nothing worth keeping.
　　'It's the extraordinary man's right—his duty—to allow his conscience to step over the obstacle of commonplace law in the execution of an idea. Moreso, if that idea involves the salvation of all mankind.'
　　Your Raskolnikov. In your *Crime and Punishment*. Taking up a hatchet and bludgeoning an old rogue to death. Determined to prove himself a man out of the ordinary.
　　Sitting in my freezing-cold room, despairing about what might be done? Your words struck me like a bolt of lightning.
FEDYA: Raskolnikov abandons that thinking.
KARAK: He abandons the idea he might be an extraordinary man—
FEDYA: You misread it—
KARAK: Not that an extraordinary man has the right to take the future in his own hands—
FEDYA: That's not what I wrote—
KARAK: But if it's what I read—?
FEDYA: Even the extraordinary man
KARAK: What we all read—
FEDYA: Must hold fast to the order of things
KARAK: Even if that order condemns us all—?
FEDYA: If Russia isn't to collapse entirely—
KARAK: You don't believe that—
FEDYA: With all my heart and soul.
KARAK: Be honest with yourself, Fyodor Mikhailovich. Why—truly—did your hero abandon his thinking?
　　Because you didn't have the courage to see it through. Because you wrote your extraordinary man and you felt liberated by the power of him. But then you got scared. You got scared. You pulled back—wrote his demise—had him kowtow to God—to salve your guilt. But it's the truth of his ideas that shine through—and will keep shining through—like fire through fog—no matter the end you contrived for him. And you'll go on writing him, this hero, until

your last breath, until you dare to acknowledge aloud the truth. That sometimes a great idea needs to be forced into being. That sometimes it's the way the world is ordered that demands we strike against it. That demands we set aside God's creation and build our own.

I learned that. I learned that at your knee as I read your work.

Surely there is here among us at least one extraordinary man.

SCENE TWENTY-FIVE

FEDYA *at the roulette wheel. A restless* MITYA *troubles* FEDYA's *imagination.*

MITYA: Drip. Drip. Drip.
    Just throw it all on and finish it.
FEDYA: It's not how it's done.
MITYA: How is it done?
FEDYA: Rigid calculation.
MITYA: Of what?
FEDYA: The past. The future.
    Play coolly. Calmly. One reckoning at a time. And it's impossible to lose.

    FEDYA *wins again—*

FEDYA: See—

But with each win he loses a little more self-control.

MITYA: You're a brave man. A brave man who dares do nothing.
FEDYA: She's with your father.
MITYA: You think you can make me kill him? Make me run there and strike his brains out? No. It's her I'd kill. Or myself. Anything to stop this craving…
    The torment of believing the woman you want is in another man's bed. The only thing, brother, we've ever had in common.

    MITYA *exits.*

In a rush, FEDYA *places his bet—it's all he has.*

The wheel stops.

SCENE TWENTY-SIX

ELENA's *flat.*

FEDYA *barges in. He is agitated.*

FEDYA: Are they lovers?
ELENA: Who?
FEDYA: Anna and Kolya.
ELENA: This is what you've rushed here to ask me?
FEDYA: Are they lovers?
ELENA: What difference to you if they are?

> *We see* MITYA *throwing rocks against the wall of his father's house.*

FEDYA: Where were you last night?
ELENA: With a man—
FEDYA: You taunt me with your men—?
ELENA: You fret about your secretary—?
FEDYA: About her loyalty—
MITYA: Where is she?

> *We hear commotion on the streets. See the shadows of people running.*

ELENA: I like to be with men who aren't scared of what Russia might be. That was you once upon a time. Or was it just your way of seducing me?
FEDYA: It was you who seduced me.
ELENA: I was an honest wife when I met you. Not an idea of straying.
FEDYA: Then you shouldn't have struck me.
ELENA: I struck you because you deserved it.
FEDYA: It was an invitation.
ELENA: A rejection.

> *A beat.*
>
> *She slaps him. She slaps him again—fiercely. He takes her.*
>
> *As they make love,* MITYA *throws the rocks more emphatically.*

MITYA: Where. Is. She?

While MITYA *continues throwing rocks, fires spread across the city.*

The fires rage.

Sounds of chaos as people panic, the LANDLADY's *broom banging incessantly against her ceiling. Her cries of God Save Us! etc.*

Then sudden, stark silence. A beat of darkness.

The sound of a ball going around a roulette wheel at a furious pace.

We see KARAKOZOV. *He has a gun—he is aiming it. He shoots.*

KARAKOZOV *surrenders.*

The LANDLADY's *broom.*

LANDLADY: [*off*] They've shot the Tsar!
Are you there, Fyodor Mikhailovich?!
They've shot the Tsar.

SCENE TWENTY-SEVEN

Pounding. Loud. Slow. Steady.

FEDYA's *flat.*

The room is in shadow.

FEDYA *sits at his table. He is lost in thought. Almost catatonic.*

MITYA *and* GRUSHENKA *together.*

MITYA: If they come…?
GRUSHENKA: They won't…
MITYA: If he's dead?
GRUSHENKA: It wasn't you.
MITYA: It's all been fixed.

No-one else will be suspected.

GRUSHENKA: You didn't kill him.

MITYA: But the freedom. The freedom I felt when I heard it was done. That he was dead. My father dead. At last. The exhilaration. Like a new life…

I wanted it. Wanted him dead. Wanted it with every cell of my being.

GRUSHENKA: You can't be hung for a wish.

FEDYA: He killed his father…

GRUSHENKA: [*to* FEDYA] He was here. With me./ I'll tell anyone who asks.

FEDYA: He killed his father. He must've done. He must have. Or I don't know what this is.

A commotion outside. Heavy footsteps. Loud voices.

The pounding, loud again. Deafening.

It morphs into the banging of the LANDLADY's *broom.*

LANDLADY: [*off*] Hide everything, Fyodor Mikhailovich! They're coming for you! They're coming!

OFFICERS *barge into the room. As they open the door, some light comes into the flat. The* OFFICERS *roughly open the shutters, lighting the room even more.*

FEDYA *is alone. He can do nothing but watch helplessly as the* OFFICERS *ransack his flat, searching through every book, every piece of paper.*

GRUSHENKA *transitions into* ELENA; MITYA *transitions into* KOLYA.

[KOLYA]: Karakozov missed.

The hand of God had intervened.

He recedes.

[ELENA]: When word that the Tsar lived made its way through the streets, the people fell down on their knees in thanks. And there they stayed.

The Commission set up to investigate the shooting—the fires—

was given unprecedented powers. And all in the name of avenging the Tsar.

She recedes.

The OFFICERS *are finished. Just* FEDYA *alone in his room. It is utter chaos.*

The banging of the broom.

LANDLADY: [*off*] Are you there, Fyodor Mikhailovich?

The broom again.

Fyodor Mikhailovich, are you alive?
FEDYA: I'm here.

A beat.

LANDLADY: [*off*] I have tea. It's hot. Come and share it.

A long beat.

FEDYA *exits.*

SCENE TWENTY-EIGHT

KOLYA'*s office.*

FEDYA *enters, sees that* ANNA *is there with* KOLYA.

FEDYA: She tells you my secrets and you tell the Third Section.
KOLYA: What are you talking about?
FEDYA: [*to* ANNA] I trusted you—
KOLYA: Stop this—
FEDYA: [*to* ANNA] How much did you tell him?
ANNA: Nothing—
FEDYA: Then why did the dogs tear my flat apart—?
KOLYA: I warned you—
FEDYA: That you'd go running to the Third Section the first chance you could—?
KOLYA: What would I tell the Third Section—?
FEDYA: [*to* ANNA] What did you tell him—?

KOLYA: What interest could I possibly have in putting your life in danger?

FEDYA: Oh, don't believe a woman's tears…

KOLYA: That mad student is likely sitting in his prison cell reeling off the names of every person he's ever met. You think your name's not going to come up?

FEDYA: [*to* ANNA] What did you tell him?

ANNA: Nothing.

A long beat. FEDYA *stares at* ANNA.

No longer able to hold his gaze, she looks away.

FEDYA: What other business do you have with him, eh? Apart from my life—?

KOLYA: She wants to help you./ We both do—

FEDYA: You were due at 10. Yet today of all days/ you stay away.

ANNA: I've been there at 10 for the last three days. And no answer./ Never an answer.

KOLYA: Because she can never find you,/ that's why she's here—

FEDYA: You knew the dogs were coming./ That they'd tear my flat apart—

KOLYA: She came here begging me to find you—

FEDYA: It's over—

ANNA: Please, Fyodor Mikhailovich—

FEDYA: Let them take all I have. Let them put me in the debtor's prison. I don't care. I don't care. If I never write another word… it's you who'll bear the blame.

FEDYA *exits.*

SCENE TWENTY-NINE

A dark alleyway. FEDYA *has no idea where he is. He is uncertain which way to go.*

ALYOSHA *is with him.*

ALYOSHA: What will happen to Mitya?

FEDYA: Let me be. I don't want this—
ALYOSHA: What will happen to him?
FEDYA: It's done. Finished.
ALYOSHA: You know where he'll be sent. You know that/ he won't survive.
FEDYA: Let. Me. Be.

I don't know what it is. I don't know what it's meant to be. What it's doing to me.

'If it's in your head to do it...'

A man can't be hung for a wish. Not for a wish. For an act, yes. An act. But not for a wish, a word. Not for a word...

It was Mitya who killed him. It had to have been. Otherwise how does it end?
ALYOSHA: He didn't kill father.
FEDYA: He killed him. He took a rock—
ALYOSHA: No—
FEDYA: He smashed it against his skull—
ALYOSHA: No—
FEDYA: He wanted him dead.
ALYOSHA: But he didn't kill him. I know.

I know.
FEDYA: Tell me. Tell me once and for all. Does God exist?
ALYOSHA: He must. Or what else are we?
FEDYA: Then is it our obligation to destroy him?
ALYOSHA: And allow all we know to collapse entirely?
FEDYA: So we risk everything on a dream? A delusion?
ALYOSHA: A hope. A promise.
FEDYA: For good? Or ill?
ALYOSHA: Good or ill is in our hands to determine.
FEDYA: And what are we? Tell me.

What do we know of the God we imagine?
ALYOSHA: Do you know what father used to say? That hanging's too good for him. The man who first invented God.

A beat.

ALYOSHA: Brother...
FEDYA: Let me be.

SCENE THIRTY

ELENA *'s flat.* ELENA *and* ANNA.

ANNA: He's sent me away. He won't open his door. He refuses to work. You understand the contract's terms?

ELENA: Perfectly.

ANNA: What he'll forfeit?

ELENA: You read them, don't you? Fedya's stories. I'd know that wide-eyed mawkishness anywhere.

You've probably devoured them since you were a child. Fallen in love with his irresolute heroes. Imagined Fedya something stepped from the pages of one of his own books.

Reality must have come as quite the shock.

ANNA: I have exhausted every other avenue…

One week's work. Less. Then he'll be free to follow whatever course he chooses.

A beat.

ELENA: I'd always envisaged Fedya and I working together. Writing together. Our ideas echoing one off the other, and the noise we would make… Deafening.

A heart as charged as my own, that's what I saw. A man I might bring to a better version of himself. Sound familiar?

You think he's listening to you… This way he has of making you believe that everything you say is entirely original. That it's never been said before, and if it has, never with such brilliance. But then, once he knows he has you, it all falls away.

ANNA: You say you love him—

ELENA: Don't you dare—

ANNA: But you'd break him as savagely/ as any creditor—

ELENA: Don't you dare to lecture me about love. What have you had—a few clumsy lovers?—and you think you know about a man like Fedya? You're a puff of air. He'd consume you, like a flame expends oxygen.

I know you're in love with him—

ANNA: No—
ELENA: I know you think he's in love with you—
ANNA: I took up stenography to pay my own way, not to attract the notice of men.
ELENA: And I'm to—what? Applaud you for putting your independence to such good use?
ANNA: Will you help him?
ELENA: Will I make him sit down with you and write this novel?
>   No.
ANNA: Then I don't know what else to do.
ELENA: You want to know what to do?
>   Walk away, Anna.
>   Walk away.
>   If you want a future that's in any way your own.

SCENE THIRTY-ONE

FEDYA's flat. In full daylight the disarray of the flat is obvious. FEDYA *sits staring at the mess.* ELENA *watches him.*

ELENA: When she told me you were refusing to work, I thought perhaps you'd seen what needed to be done. Yet here you are. Still as a statue.
FEDYA: Did you think you could push and push? That the Tsar wouldn't/ dig in his heels?
ELENA: It wasn't me who turned your flat upside down. And it wasn't the students. And it wasn't because someone took a shot at the Tsar that it was done, though they'll use it as their excuse. You thought the freedoms you'd won were secure? Not when it takes just the whim of one man and his futile government to tighten again the leash and wrench us all back into line.

>   *A beat.*

ELENA: The day the first of the shots were fired. That's the day you finally called me back to you.
>   You wanted to be part of this. You wanted that we should be part of this together.

You cannot lose your nerve.
FEDYA: Where, Elena? Where in all this destruction does a spirit breathe?
ELENA: You think there's room for the spirit in what we have? When all is put to right—there'll be room enough for the spirit then.
FEDYA: For the few who survive the guns.
ELENA: Which is the greater sin, Fedya? To wither away—surrender the essence of yourself—for want of action? Or to dare to build something new—and bear the sacrifices that must be made?

Karakozov put himself forward. He put his life forward. For the good of us all.
FEDYA: What is it you want me to do? What?
ELENA: It's not Russia you fear for Fedya. All this disquiet about blood and destruction. No. It's your own life that obsesses you. Of dying without ever becoming this man you seem to believe yourself to be.
FEDYA: It's not death that scares me.
ELENA: What then?
FEDYA: Losing my soul.
ELENA: You have no soul to lose. It's an idea that's past its time. Just another of your maudlin—
FEDYA: You know nothing of me—
ELENA: Another of your maudlin—
FEDYA: You know nothing of me—
ELENA: You really think we can have been lovers this long—
FEDYA: You know nothing of who I am!
ELENA: Because you refuse to share yourself with me.
FEDYA: And all you'll get you have.

A long beat.

ELENA *readies to leave.*

ELENA: Sit here and do nothing if you must. But there's a boy in the fortress who is being tortured—
FEDYA: Who brought him here? Who trailed him around Petersburg like a dog?

How many of us must dance and dance and fall at your feet before you see what you do?

ELENA: You're a louse. A louse. A scrap of life that barely deserves our attention. You're nothing like a man.

    ELENA *is almost out the door.*

FEDYA: You know why I gamble?

ELENA: Enlighten me.

FEDYA: Because gamble all you have and you understand. That there's something absurd in us. Irrational. And no matter how much you will it otherwise, it won't be suppressed.

ELENA: Because you can't quell the irrational in yourself?

FEDYA: It won't work. Your way. It can't work.

    There's nothing—nothing—that will make men love their fellow-men. There's no law of nature that demands it. That man should love mankind.

ELENA: Watch the next turn of the wheel, Fedya. You'll see how wrong you are.

SCENE THIRTY-TWO

The actor playing ELENA, *getting out of costume.*

[ELENA]: We'll never be their equal. We'll always wants more of them than they'll ever want of us.

    People will know that Fedya and I once loved. He will give his account of it, and I'll give mine. Let the scholars debate as long as they will whose version is the truth and whose the work of genius.

SCENE THIRTY-THREE

KOLYA'*s office. A dishevelled* FEDYA *has just arrived. He has a crumpled page in his hands.*

FEDYA: [*referring to the page*] Spare not the guilty?

KOLYA: If I'm to survive,/ what choice do I have—?

FEDYA: Spare not the guilty?

KOLYA: If the alternative is to leave the rest of us defenceless? Then yes, 'spare not the guilty'.

Since when does progressive politics mean standing back while decent people are terrorised and hounded to death?

A long beat.

FEDYA: I need money.

KOLYA: That's all you have to say?

FEDYA: Karakozov is to be executed.

KOLYA: While those who provoked him flee.

I pity him.

FEDYA holds out his hand.

FEDYA: I'll never be free while I'm forever burdened by debts.

Finish what you've started, Kolya. Put me out of my misery once and for all. But tell them everything this time.

KOLYA: You want to keep the Third Section off your back? Work. Write your novels. Meet your contract—

FEDYA: You haven't seen what they've done!

This isn't opening my mail. Watching where I go. Knocking on my door at all hours of the night. They've turned my apartment upside down. I don't know what they've taken, I don't know what they've left behind…

KOLYA: What was there?

FEDYA: You know/ there's nothing.

KOLYA: How do I know what you have/ hidden away there?

FEDYA: Nothing. I have nothing.

KOLYA: Then what does it matter what they've taken—

FEDYA: Because it's my work! My work! It's all I have!

A long beat.

FEDYA: I could pinpoint every sheet of paper. Every chapter, annotation. Every thought, but… I don't know now. The confusion of it all. I don't know whether to toss every last sheet of it on to the fire or to believe there really might be something amongst it all that's worth saving.

A long beat.

KOLYA: I didn't betray you, Fedya. I have never betrayed you.

FEDYA: Give me money.

KOLYA *puts money on the desk.*

FEDYA: You gave me up.
KOLYA: It wasn't me.
FEDYA: You gave us all up.
KOLYA: If you need to believe that—
FEDYA: Released with not a mark/ against your name—
KOLYA: In order to bleed me dry/ with your endless empty promises of novels and articles—
FEDYA: Released with compensation—
KOLYA: Then fine. Go on. I'll bear it. Because I believe in the man you might one day be. And I would sacrifice anything—anything…
I didn't betray you.
FEDYA: Friend—God—Tsar, Kolya. If we don't interrogate their every word. Their every silence. Then what use are we?

FEDYA *takes the money. Exits.*

SCENE THIRTY-FOUR

The actor playing KOLYA *getting out of costume.*

[KOLYA]: I was young. And to be among such people? To be counted a friend by Dostoyevsky? Who wouldn't have boasted…? Who wouldn't have ventured—perhaps once, perhaps twice—to repeat what they'd heard—feel the shiver of such words on their own tongue? Who wouldn't have risked another man's name to advance their own?

SCENE THIRITY-FIVE

The beating sound of heavy rain.

FEDYA *at the roulette tables. He is agitated. He is losing.*

In his imagination, he can see a figure cowering in the corner of a cell. It may be KARAKOZOV. *It may be* ALYOSHA. *He can hardly tell them apart.*

SCENE THIRTY-SIX

ANNA's *flat.* ANNA *stands with a wet, bedraggled* FEDYA.

FEDYA: You judge me.

ANNA: No.

FEDYA: You have no comprehension what it's like. After ten years in Siberia—after proving yourself to be a man of character—strength—and yet to still find within yourself a need of such force—to stand before fate and throw all you have on whatever way out it might offer you—a need so intense…

It's as though the world is offering you the chance to breathe again. If only for a moment.

ANNA: What do you want, Fyodor Mikhailovich?

FEDYA: I need to meet this contract.

ANNA: What does that have to do with me any more?

FEDYA: I need your help.

ANNA: I've taken another job.

You should go home. Get dry—

FEDYA: I can't go home—

ANNA: Why?

FEDYA: I can't—

ANNA: Why not?

FEDYA: Are you lovers?

ANNA: How could you/ even ask—?

FEDYA: Did he pay you—?

ANNA: Stop—

FEDYA: To tell him what I'd done—?

ANNA: Stop—

FEDYA: To tell him I'm more guilty than even he could have imagined—?

ANNA: Stop!

FEDYA: You don't know him, Anna.

ANNA: I don't know you.

I used to think the world of you—once upon a time.

Go home.

FEDYA: He's there. He's there all the time. He follows me.

ANNA: Who's there?

FEDYA: I think it was him. Who killed his father? Not directly, not by his own hand, but...
ANNA: Who? Who killed his father?
FEDYA: In my story. Of the parricide.
There's a third brother. I see it now. He's a revolutionary. A true revolutionary. An atheist for whom it's more than just a political stance. Who sees nothing but emptiness. And I've heard his voice in my head. Day and night. 'In God is nothing. In God is nothing.' But it's not so much God that he rejects as the world God's created. Can see no alternative than that it must all come crashing down. And the accident of man's existence, that he has no other purpose but to watch its disintegration.
There's a painting—in Basel I think it is—and I've made him, this brother, I've made him stand in front of it. For hours. Just contemplating it. It's of Christ. The dead Christ. His corpse. He was shaken to his very soul. To see Christ there—a man like any other. All bone and shrunken flesh. And his face horror-struck by the wrench of his last moment. As though not a breath of divinity or resurrection would ever move through him. It terrified him—this brother—to see everything he'd ever argued so forcefully proven that it could never again be doubted...
ANNA: If this is the man you must write, then... then you must write him.
FEDYA: It has driven him mad.
ANNA: Then you must find him his salvation.
FEDYA: I can't.
I need to meet this contract.
Help me.

SCENE THIRTY-SEVEN

ANNA *putting on coat, hat, gloves etc, readying herself for work.*

ANNA: It wasn't, I told myself, that I couldn't live without him, but that I couldn't live without playing such a part... Without touching, in the frailest way, all that he might one day write—all that he might one day be...

SCENE THIRTY-EIGHT

FEDYA*'s flat. There are still papers everywhere.* ANNA *is very business-like, gathering her own notes together.*

ANNA: I'll have them transcribed and returned to you first thing tomorrow.

FEDYA: It's done then?

ANNA: One hundred and fifty pages.

FEDYA: Is it any good, Anna?

ANNA: I'm not here to judge the worth of what you write, Fyodor Mikhailovich.

A beat.

FEDYA: Would you like tea?

ANNA: No.

FEDYA: We hardly stopped—

ANNA: I'd like to get home—

FEDYA: Your hand—

ANNA: Is fine.

FEDYA: [*gathering together his scraps of paper*] Is it really all over…?

ANNA *busies herself packing her bag.*

A quiet pounding.

FEDYA *shifts towards the state that precedes a fit.*

The pounding gets louder.

Tightening spotlight on FEDYA. *Building spotlight on a* SOLDIER, *standing in the snow. He is cold. He has a rifle. His feet, the rifle, pound on the ground as he tries to stay warm.*

We see the whole room again.

ANNA: Fyodor Mikhailovich—

The pounding sound again.

Spotlight on FEDYA. *Spotlight on the same* SOLDIER, *standing in the snow. Still pounding his rifle, pounding his feet, trying to stay warm.*

We see the whole room again.

What can I do?

A crack like a gunshot.

In that moment, almost like a flash—

Tight spotlight on FEDYA. *Another tight light on* KARAKOZOV. *Another on the* SOLDIER. *All the lights are incredibly bright.*

Another crack. KARAKOZOV *is shot. He falls.*

We see the whole room again. We hear the LANDLADY*'s broom banging.*

LANDLADY: [*off*] They've executed him, Fyodor Mikhailovich. That bastard student is dead.

Another crack.

In that moment, like a flash—

Tight spotlight on FEDYA. *Incredibly bright. Tight spotlight on the* SOLDIER, *his gun aimed at* FEDYA. FEDYA *waits for it to fire. The* SOLDIER *fires into the air.*

We see the whole room again.

ANNA: Fyodor Mikhailovich—
What can I do?

The room is overwhelmed by shadows.

Reality gives way to FEDYA*'s imagination.*

The moment where the two worlds of the play merge: he is unsure whether it is ANNA *or* KATYA *who is standing in front of him; he is the third brother in his novel of the parricide, speaking to the woman he refuses to admit he loves.*

FEDYA: Why do I cling to it? This misery?

Because it's the substance of my life—forever suspended between belief and disbelief... God and...

If you could sow within me one grain of faith... one grain—if we could live for this world alone... But with all we know—the more we know—there can be no truth. No truth. It changes from one day to the next and...

A man sees such things, such a complex reality, such events, a whole world of events, woven into such a plot, full of such astonishing details, beginning with the most exalted manifestations of the human spirit to the last button on a dress front...

He is close to ANNA/KATYA *now. An intensely intimate moment.*

The blood's still here. The blood's still on my hands. How is it I'm left to live? When I too wanted him dead? When I'm as guilty as him?

The light holds for a moment. Seeps to a deep blood red.

We see the whole room again.

FEDYA *falls to his knees.*

The first moments of a fit.

Darkness.

Then silence.

SCENE THIRTY-NINE

A light in the darkness. A small fire burning.

FEDYA*'s flat.*

FEDYA *is asleep on the sofa.*

ANNA *is tidying the room—she has made a few inroads into the mess, though the disarray is still evident.*

FEDYA *stirs.*

FEDYA: I thought you were leaving.
ANNA: Today. I'm leaving today.
FEDYA: The novel?
ANNA: Taken to the notary.
FEDYA: Not to Stellovsky?
ANNA: He couldn't be found.
>   The notary has it. He knows your side of the bargain was kept.
>
>   *A beat.*
>
> I found your notebook. The one you were asking for.
> Here.
>
> *She hands him his notebook. He riffles through the pages.*

FEDYA: How do I write, Anna?
>   How do I turn what's in my head into words? Words that warrant an ounce of anyone's attention?

ANNA: You sit at your desk, Fyodor Mikhailovich. You put your pen to the paper.
>   FEDYA *tears pages from the notebook, throws them on to the fire.*

ANNA: Fyodor Mikhailovich—?
FEDYA: It's not what I thought it was.
ANNA: So you destroy it?
FEDYA: If there's anything in it—anything of merit—a fire's not going to destroy it.
>   *A long beat.*

ANNA: [*gathering her things to leave*] I'll ask the landlady to bring you soup. Whatever you need.
FEDYA: I had a dream, Anna Grigorevna. A good dream it seemed. A dream that seemed to promise good things. I was organising my papers. Trying to. Amongst all the mess I found the strangest thing. Buried underneath piles and piles of papers. A tiny diamond. Tiny. But with such a fierce light. I knew I'd treasure it to the end of my days.
>   What do you think it might mean?

ANNA: A dream is a dream.
FEDYA: I'm wrong to think it might herald some happiness to come?

ANNA: Elena Petrovna is a very beautiful woman. I'm sure she'll bring you great happiness.

FEDYA: Elena has gone to Paris. I don't expect ever to see her again.

A beat.

FEDYA: I thought I might work it into a novel. A pitiable man who dreams of such a treasure. Who spends all his life searching for it. Who ends by discovering it's been in the one place—the one place closest to his heart—where he has always failed to look.

Would you believe that possible, Anna? If you read such a novel?

ANNA: In the pages of a novel… yes, I'd believe it.

But I feel you're teasing me, sir—

FEDYA: Sir?

ANNA: Playing with me—

FEDYA: Why would I do that?

ANNA: To judge how a young woman—an inexperienced woman, if you will—might react to such words.

FEDYA: How would she react?

ANNA: I don't know how to unriddle you—

FEDYA: How would she react?

ANNA: I could work for you every day for the rest of my life and I'd never understand you.

FEDYA: Tell me, Anna. How?

ANNA: I don't know. What do I know? What does she know? But that this man was four weeks ago—four days ago—on fire with such a passion… That he would watch this other woman walk into the room and the desire that would… What do I know? But that I have been abused and tried and tested… So much good… So much good, Fyodor Mikhailovich has been crushed out of me. Crushed out of all of us. Between these bombs and executions and hatreds that speak nothing of my life. It seems impossible to know anymore—what is right. What is good. It seems that it's only in the pages of a novel that anything good can survive. That hope can survive.

You tested me—

FEDYA: No—

ANNA: You tested my loyalty to you—

FEDYA: No—

ANNA: What did you want? Did you want me to betray you? And now, is it that I'm supposed to deny you—?

FEDYA: Deny me?

ANNA: To give you yet another thing to mourn for—?

FEDYA: It wasn't to test you—

ANNA: Another excuse to do nothing, to run from all you might achieve—?

FEDYA: To test my fate. My fate. To see if the past would be allowed to rest. Or if it would rise up and bury me.

ANNA: What do you want me to do? Just say. Do you want to live, Fyodor Mikhailovich? Or do you want to die?

FEDYA: Before I fell ill—in the clear moments that come before the darkness—I was again in front of the firing squad, Anna… waiting for the order to fire. And an abyss opened out at my feet. A chance to save myself. I knew I must jump—could see no other answer but to jump. But I couldn't move. Not from the fear of it—the fear of not making it to the other side—but because of all I wasn't yet prepared to abandon. It was trading one manner of freedom for another. One manner of imprisonment. I was frozen to the spot…

It became clear to me then. Clear as it had never been before. What I must write. How I must live. It was a revelation. That I can live again. That even among the darkest and ugliest aspects of life, I can live. As long as my soul is free—as long as my mind is not captive…

Agreeing to life, Anna—agreeing to God—they're acts of will. Like forgiveness. Like love.

ANNA: Forgiveness can't be deliberated, Fyodor Mikhailovich. Nor love. We can only answer what's in our hearts.

A long beat.

FEDYA: Could she love him, Anechka?

Could she?

A beat.

ANNA *leads him back to the table. Sits him down. Hands him a new notebook, a pen.*

A beat.

He returns to the fire, salvages a page or two of the notebook, takes them back with him to the desk.

As ANNA *continues to work to bring order to the flat,*

FEDYA *bends his head, begins to write.*

THE END

www.ingramcontent.com/pod-product-compliance
Lightning Source LLC
Chambersburg PA
CBHW040307170426
43194CB00022B/2929